DATE DUE			

Violence & Democracy

Other Books by the Authors

BY JONATHAN B. BINGHAM

Shirtsleeve Diplomacy: Point Four in Action

BY ALFRED M. BINGHAM

Insurgent America: Revolt of the Middle Classes
Man's Estate: Adventures in Economic Discovery
The United States of Europe
The Techniques of Democracy

Vio
Dem

Jonathan B. Bingha

The World Publishing Company

New York and Cleveland

ence &
ocracy

nd Alfred M. Bingham

EXCALIBUR BOOKS

Carl Hermann Voss, Editor

Published by The World Publishing Company
110 East 59th Street, New York, New York 10022
Published simultaneously in Canada by
Nelson, Foster & Scott Ltd.
Library of Congress catalog card number: 71–101857
Copyright © 1970 by The World Publishing Company.
Designed by Jacques Chazaud

Contents

Violence & Democracy

Part One

A Generation in Revolt

1 "Spring of Hope, Winter of Despair"

It was the best of times, it was the worst of times, it was the age of wisdom, it was the age of foolishness, it was the epoch of belief, it was the epoch of incredulity, it was the season of Light, it was the season of Darkness, it was the spring of hope, it was the winter of despair, we had everything before us, we had nothing before us, we were all going directly to Heaven, we were all going direct the other way—in short, the period was so far like the present period, that some of its noisiest authorities insisted on its being received, for good or for evil, in the superlative degree of comparison only.

So Charles Dickens, at the beginning of *A Tale of Two Cities,* described the Western world as it had appeared just before the American and French revolutions. He was looking back almost a hundred years. He might have been describing our own time, a hundred years later.

The decade of the 1970's has opened with extravagant expectations. Middle-aged commentators confess to despair over the future of this overcrowded and violent planet. Young radicals are even more certain of doom, though they expect a new world to rise from the ashes of the old.

Seeing the earth from the moon has given to millions a new perspective on our common fate. They are appalled at the poverty of most of their fellow humans. From the Black Belt of the South, from Appalachia and the farm labor camps of California come pictures of the matchstick legs and bloated stomachs of starving children. At the core of every big American city are corruption and misery. A few hours away, in the Caribbean, in Latin America, in Africa and Asia, millions are being born only to die of hunger. Why, then, should there not be despair, unrest, revolution and talk of revolution?

Yet the pessimists are faced with paradox. Never has mankind been so well off. The mass unemployment and economic depression that had wracked the world a generation earlier have yielded to new understanding of economic processes. Today's crises are the crises of prosperity: inflation, waste, pollution, pockets of poverty next door to unseemly wealth, rich nations growing too fast, poor nations lagging even farther behind. The United States has poured billions into foreign aid and technical assistance to backward areas, and billions into a war on poverty at home. Have people ever attempted to do more for their neighbors?

No good intentions are recognized, however, by the young radicals who have been calling for revolution. They see poverty not relieved, but caused, by the rich and powerful, by a system of corporate greed which ruthlessly consumes natural and human resources at home while waging genocidal war against non-white peoples abroad. They see a monstrous Frankenstein piling up enough doomsday machines to wipe out life on a dozen planets, let alone just our own.

Yet again there seems ground for optimism. A quarter of a century has passed since World War II and there is no World War III. The great powers, if not grown humble, are at least no longer arrogant, and are more concerned to damp down brush-fire wars than to fan them. A whole family of international and regional organizations has become part of the world scene, providing a foundation on which to build eventually a system of world peace through law. Even Vietnam can be seen as a kind of anachronistic reminder of a doomed system of colonial empires that the white man once liked to call his "burden."

That is small comfort for those who fear their lives may be snuffed out before they are fairly started. Extinction by multitargeted thermonuclear weaponry, or by a sniper's bullet, or in a raid on a Black Panther headquarters, may for the man extinguished be all the same. On one point the new generation and their elders can agree: the times are violent.

Whether the violence is more or less than in times past is beside the point. What about the future? Nuclear bombs have not been dropped on people since Hiroshima and Nagasaki, but a thousand cities are now targeted for incineration, with the delivery vehicles held only on a tenuous leash. Accidental deaths on American highways continue to rise, and in a single holiday weekend they can surpass the casualties incurred in all the ghetto riots, campus confrontations, and demonstrations for peace and civil rights of the turbulent 1960's. As crimes of violence and talk of guerrilla warfare have mounted, so has the sale of guns to householders. Many Americans for the first time are double-bolting their doors, and are afraid to venture on the streets at night.

What is the prospect for the 1970's, when in New York City, the business capital of the world and the seat of the United Nations, tens of thousands of teen-agers are becoming drug addicts, dependent on mugging and robbery to support their addiction? Vandalism and violence in the city's schools have reached the point where teachers seek police protection in the corridors. New schools, to save the cost of replacing broken windows, are designed windowless. Gang violence is not peculiar to the big cities: visitations by black-jacketed Hell's Angels on motorcycles are dreaded in California villages, and their counterparts can be found from Maine to Florida, and, in a world grown small, from Sweden to the Riviera.

Mounting disorder in America was investigated by two presidential commissions at the end of the decade of the sixties. The rioting, looting, and burning in the big city ghettos, which reached its highest point in the summer of 1967, led to the creation of the Kerner

Commission on Civil Disorders. Then in 1968 the shooting of Martin Luther King and Robert Kennedy, latest in what seemed an accelerating series of political assassinations, prompted the setting up of the National Commission on the Causes and Prevention of Violence.

Both commissions emphasized the role of the young. The Kerner Commission found that "the rioters were late teen-agers or young adults." The subsequent commission under the chairmanship of Milton Eisenhower, reported that:

> "the key to much of the violence in our society seems to lie with the young. Our youth account for an ever-increasing percentage of crime, greater than their increasing percentage of the population. The thrust of much of the group protest and collective violence—on the campus, in the ghettos, in the streets—is provided by our young people."

There might be general agreement that most of the violent are young. But is there any reason to link a youthful bank robber with a militant student taking over a university president's office in a protest demonstration? Is a black teen-ager throwing a firebomb through a Cleveland shop window a juvenile delinquent or a "freedom fighter"? What is the difference between crime and civil disobedience?

The old and the young will give different answers. Conservatives tend to see the turmoil of the 1960's as a general breakdown of respect for authority. In the belief that too much license has been granted the young, they call for a crackdown, not only on criminals, but also on student demonstrators and black militants. They have in mind the warnings of those political philosophers of the past who saw the people as a great beast, feared the tyranny of the majority, and equated democracy with mob rule. Liberals, on the other hand, have answered that we have too little freedom, too little democracy. They have called for massive programs to end poverty, rebuild the cities, eliminate racial injustice; they see the violence as a sign of the need for reform.

Among the young, an increasing number, particularly those who have been involved in group violence, have come to believe that our society, behind a mask of democracy, is based on violence—police violence at home and war abroad. They believe that a system maintained by force can be changed only by force. Some even glorify violence as the harbinger of a bright new day.

These are the revolutionaries. Far more numerous, indeed most of a generation, are those who are no less in revolt, yet hate violence. They may not know about the power structure, but they fear the police. Their revolt is not against political institutions, though they have little use for them, but against the manners and morals of their elders. If a revolution is in the making it may be shaped more by those who have been feeling their way to new cultural and moral standards than by those who proclaim themselves revolutionists.

Many have asserted their separateness by certain conventions of hair, clothing, speech. The more dedicated marchers of the civil rights and peace movements have adopted the same conventions to signify their break with the past. The underworld of the disturbed and the delinquent has often expressed its defiance of society by similar mannerisms. In essence it was the hippie style that symbolized the cultural revolt of the 1960's.

To the "squares" of an older generation the gap seemed appallingly wide. The beards, sandals, and strings of beads were an affront to smooth-shaven fathers in gray flannel suits, as were the girls' untidy hair and dirty bare feet to their well-groomed mothers. Even more disturbing was the substitution of occult mysteries for the certainties of the stock market report, and of hashish for the evening cocktail.

The break with the past was perhaps more apparent than real. Buddha and Jesus and Francis of Assisi were all in their way rebels against material wealth and the Establishment, and their followers went robed and barefoot. Cults of mysticism and piety have outraged the authorities in other times of social upheaval. And the use of mind-changing drugs to induce states of ecstasy is at least as old as the cult of Dionysos.

The more recent antecedents of the present cultural revolution were in the 1920's. The first World War shattered the illusions and the pieties of the Victorian era. Hemlines went up, and barriers to women's rights came down. Ernest Hemingway fled to Paris to escape American normalcy, while Sinclair Lewis stayed to satirize Main Street and Babbittry. Young people shocked their parents as much by their taste for cubism and Dadaism as by their interest in bathtub gin and the Charleston. In Europe, where battle deaths had wiped out a whole generation, new cults of youth appeared. In Italy some had romantic notions of purification by violence, and marched to the tune of *Giovinezza*, the Fascist hymn of youth. In Germany the *Wandervögel*, the hitchhikers and easy-riders of their day, sang folk songs under the stars, until Hitler inspired them with his vision of "strength through joy." In the countries bled white by victory, young people asked why their fathers had died, and Oxford students took a pledge never again to fight "for king and country."

While some were turning to pacifism and some to fascism, other young people were deeply stirred by the Russian Revolution. Communism seemed to offer answers for the doubts, frustrations and discontents of the alienated young: whether it was bourgeois art and morals they objected to, or poverty and unemployment, or the horrors of war, all could be blamed on the capitalist system, and only when the ruling class had been overthrown by revolution could a new social order be built.

Revolutionary hopes and dreams of a better world were laid aside when that generation went to war in its turn. In the numbing aftermath of World War II it seemed for a while as if all the world were middle-aged. It was the world of Eisenhower and Dulles, Khrushchev and Mao Tse-tung, a world of ever more massive organization and calculated but unthinking power. But there was a Third World, a world of the black and brown, where the revolution went on, in the form of anti-colonial independence movements and "wars of liberation," with a feedback to a new generation of rebels in the developed countries.

In Paris, young people began once more to protest as they were called up to die for an outworn empire in Indo-China and Algeria. Some of them found an answer, though a bleak one, in the existentialist philosophies of Albert Camus and Jean-Paul Sartre, for whom the world held little meaning except in struggle against cruelty and oppression.

Another feedback came to young blacks in the ghettos of America, who began to believe for the first time that the world was not destined always to be ruled by whites.

In music a kind of black cultural identity had survived slavery and discrimination: rhythmic beats, mournful chants, blues, and jazz. Other expressions of resentment against the rich and powerful had long lingered in the folk ballads of the European immigrants as they moved west. Some of these strains of popular music nourished the spirit of revolt during the doldrums of the 1950's, when liberals and radicals of an earlier period were retreating before Joe McCarthy, and bewailing the apathy of the younger generation.

When the postwar dropouts and the disaffected began to let their hair grow, when they hit the road and set a noticeable style, their elders saw them as failures and called them beatniks. The Sputniks had, by the late 1950's, shocked the Establishment with the threat of a superior Russian technology, and universities were being urged to expand their scientific disciplines. But the beatniks claimed they felt not beaten but beatific, as their experiments with mind-changing drugs liberated them from convention, and new states of consciousness opened before them.

With the beginning of the 1960's, it seemed to many of the young that the initiative had indeed passed to them, though with a style that linked the new with the best of the past: a young President declared at his inauguration that a new generation was now in command. The revolt of youth came near to being co-opted. Even the ghettos might never have exploded if John Kennedy had lived.

Instead, public life returned to rule by middle-aged men and middle-aged ideas. The restlessness of the young found expression in the insistent beat of rock 'n' roll. Now the Liverpool sound of the Beatles was added to the other strains of the music of rebellion.

And with the Beatles came not just new songs but a sudden popularization of the new life modes. It began to transform not only the American scene but all of western Europe and Japan, and then to reach through to the Communist world; even the Third World emerging from colonialism felt its impact.

Young people with long hair, carrying electric guitars, helped shape the patterns of revolt that brought violence and talk of revolution to the American ghetto and the campus, and even a symbolic assault on the Pentagon.

A modern Rip Van Winkle coming down out of the Catskills in the summer of 1969 after a twenty-year sleep would have wondered whether he or the world had gone mad. The country roads near the little village of Bethel, New York, were clogged with people. Many were in cars, but the cars were bumper to bumper, and not moving. Thousands were walking, along the sides of the roads, or scrambling across the fields. They were almost all young, but some of them were as bearded as Rip Van Winkle himself. They were uncouth, often ragged and dirty. Their language was as uncouth as their dress.

The Woodstock Rock Festival was not the first festival of rock music but it was then the biggest, and the most astonishing to the older generation who observed or read about it. The new "life style" which expressed itself in dress and manners and language was so universal as to seem standardized. The music which had drawn the crowd—though many never got to hear it because of the congestion on the roads—was loud and sensual. Vast sums had been spent in hiring performers, building a huge stage, and promoting what was intended to be a gigantic enterprise—though not as gigantic as it turned out to be—yet the young people might have been in a primitive wilderness. The rains came, and the farm fields turned to mud, and warm bodies huddled in cars or in tents or even out under the dripping skies.

Yet most of the reports were of a happiness, a euphoria, due in part, no doubt, to the nearly universal use of marijuana and other drugs, but also to a wonderful sense of togetherness.

There was little organization, no authority, a mob without discipline, virtual anarchy over an area of several square miles. Good nature and easy accommodation prevailed and there was practically no violence. Even local residents and the police, who would have been overwhelmed if any major disturbance had occurred, spoke of the amiability of the young participants.

This was an outpouring of close to half a million young people, consciously or unconsciously asserting that they had broken with the past. They felt a sense of triumph in their sheer numbers. Here was the revolution already arrived, and happily uncomplicated by violence.

Six months later, at the Altamont rock festival in California, the "vibrations" were more ominous. There was brutal violence as well as euphoria. Members of the motorcycle gang of Hell's Angels were paid to keep order, and suppressed one disruptive celebrant by killing him. The new generation has potentialities for cruelty as well as gentleness, for cynicism as well as love.

At both festivals, paradox was plain. The songs were of simplicity and love and honesty and doing your own thing, in rejection not only of an older generation, but of a whole civilization. Yet the singers have made millions from recordings and television. The simple folk music, no less than the latest acid rock, was more electronic than human. Many of the young people who came to listen drove the family car. Yet, even if the times in which they live have been good to them in material ways, the young don't believe in them.

In part, to be sure, the revolution is only a matter of style. The young have often been in the vanguard in styles of dress, hair-dos, and personal mannerisms, and their elders have now also begun to let their hair grow and develop sideburns, or go without bras and make-up.

In part, too, hair and drugs and rock music are merely symbolic assertions of independence from parental discipline. The same might have been said of the rejection of bourgeois propriety and bourgeois taste that earlier bohemians had expressed in Greenwich Village or on the Paris Left Bank.

Yet there is more than a traditional generation gap, or a disdain for conventional esthetics, in the new ways of living. The long hair may well be as much a symbol of revolutionary change as the short hair of the Roundheads in Cromwell's day.

The younger generation has lost its faith in the established culture, the modern world—what is called western civilization.

The young hardly know why they have lost faith in it, and they have little idea what they would have in its place. Their rejection is not one of understanding but of bafflement. The world is too big, too complicated. Its operations are so specialized, the scientific explanation of the natural world has become so esoteric, the social order has become so computerized, that the young are unable to see the meaning in an existence that their parents can still believe in.

Life, for many an intelligent youngster today, is only a happening.

The modern age began when faith in reason began to replace faith in God. The idea of progress inspired the American dream, which has dominated our national culture. Progress is still in the official creed, and when astronauts planted the American flag on the moon's surface at a cost of twenty-five billion dollars, it was clear that there were still plenty of believers. But the fact that so many of the young don't feel this is their world is a portent. It may not mean the kind of revolution which some of the young now speak about so confidently. But it does portend a crisis in human affairs. And the evidence of youthful unbelief and revolt in almost all the countries of the globe suggests that this is a crisis of the world's culture and not of America's alone.

In Piccadilly Circus, around the fountain of love, hurrying London shoppers and clerks and passing American tourists may see the hippies vacantly watching the world go by. In other European capitals, and even in distant Kathmandu, the drug-glazed eyes of the flower children stare at their alien elders. Across a cultural gap, if not a generation gap, each sees the other as a denizen of another planet.

Other periods of social change have been marked by similar other-worldly cults. What is new is to have this search for meaning in the universe at the very time that the older faith, in material progress through science, seems, with man's escape from gravity itself, to have achieved the ultimate triumph.

Yet even the astronauts' great venture into space betrayed elements of absurdity along with old-fashioned courage and scientific genius. The confining discomforts of life in a rocket ship and the curious kangaroo hops of the first men on the moon, watched live on TV by a hundred million earthlings, raised doubts of the meaning of progress.

Some of the young have given up looking for the meaning of anything. Zen Buddhism and existentialist philosophy have enabled them to make a virtue of the absurdity of the human predicament. They find meaning in meaninglessness, the theater of the absurd, new forms of pop art. They have tried to create a politics of absurdity: the Youth International Party, the "Yippies," nominated a pig for President during the Chicago Democratic Convention in 1968.

Yet in spite of evident absurdities, the revolt of youth has not been without success in finding meanings, and in spite of what often appears as shocking immorality, in the drug culture, nudity, exhibitionism, violence, it is a profoundly moral revolt.

2 | Black Revolt

In the summer of 1964 three young civil rights workers were murdered in Mississippi, and their bodies were buried in an earth dam. Two of them were white and one was black. They were participants in the Mississippi Summer Project, under which student volunteers, mostly from Northern campuses, invaded the Southern stronghold of white supremacy in support of a drive to get Negroes registered as voters. The campaign was initiated by the Student Nonviolent Coordinating Committee (SNCC, pronounced "Snick"), an organization started by Negro students but including whites in its leadership and membership, and by young militants from the recently formed Congress of Racial Equality (CORE).

The civil rights movement, which had been gathering momentum since the Supreme Court decision outlawing segregation in the schools in 1954, was at its peak. Freedom Rides in buses and sit-ins in restaurants had been deliberate violations of local ordinances and state laws, and participants had faced imprisonment as well as beatings by police and angry mobs. But federal courts had freed the lawbreakers and held all Jim Crow laws unconstitutional. At Little Rock, Arkansas, and Oxford, Mississippi, and in dozens of Southern towns and cities, the power of the United States Government, even its armed might, had been needed to overcome resistance, of varying degrees of

25

violence. But the Constitution and the rule of law had been upheld, and the successes achieved by a movement committed to non-violence gave promise that the American democratic system was capable of achieving even profound social change peacefully.

For many white Americans—and, after all, nine out of ten Americans considered themselves white—the murder of these young civil rights workers was a soul-searing event.

Not that murder of young men was unprecedented. John Fitzgerald Kennedy, the youngest President ever elected, had been assassinated six months before, but that was an isolated crime, and for all the fear of a possible conspiracy, it still seemed to present no threat to the peace and stability of the country. Young Medgar Evers, leader of the NAACP in Mississippi, had been shot and killed earlier that year, and three little girls had died in the bombing of a Birmingham church, but they were black. Had all three of the murdered civil rights workers been black, white America would not have been so aroused. As it was, white America felt a shudder of apprehension. Was a new Civil War in the offing? Was the end of racial discrimination, after all, so profound a social change that it could come about only through violence?

But that these questions should be raised by white Americans only because white Americans had been killed was a cause for black rage. Violence against men of black skin for resisting white supremacy was commonplace, and murder of blacks, whether in spectacular lynchings or by police or by individual white men, had gone unpunished for generations. With the arousal of a substantial part of white America to the frightening potentialities of the civil rights movement came a new awareness of the gulf between blacks and whites. Even within the civil rights movement, it was becoming difficult for blacks and whites to understand one another or to work together.

In the South the gulf seemed unbridgeable. Both blacks and whites were buying guns and stocking ammunition. Many white Southerners believed their previously docile black neighbors were being misled by evil-minded communists and hippies. They felt it quite possible that a massive uprising of the black population, which in some Southern counties constituted a majority of the population, would involve a direct attack on their lives and property and womenfolk. Even if mass violence were not initiated by the blacks, the revived Ku Klux Klan was rapidly growing in strength, arming its members, and preparing for violent resistance. A blood bath seemed imminent.

With the migration of Negroes from newly mechanized Southern farms to Northern cities becoming a flood, Southern segregationists, who were encouraging and assisting it, hoped the North would come to agree with the South on the necessity of maintaining white supremacy. They counted on law and order to restrain the kind of violence threatened by the Klan. But could anyone restrain the rising militancy of the civil rights movement?

The 1954 Supreme Court school decision had done more than change the interpretation of the Constitution. It had released long repressed impulses to violent rebellion. At the time, to all except Southern whites, the decision had seemed a triumph of peaceful reform through the democratic process. Now the nearness of massive violence shocked the whole country, particularly complacent liberals of an older generation, to a new awareness of the fragility of democracy. And young idealists began to wonder whether fundamental social change was possible without violent struggle. They were losing confidence in a generation of social reformers who had taken the submerged black population so much for granted as scarcely to include their problems in schemes for social improvement. Some white students, joining the struggle for racial equality, were coming to believe that the whole American way of life, behind a false front of benevolence, was organized repression.

For two hundred years before Lincoln said this country was "dedicated to the proposition that all men are created equal," and to "government of the people, by the people, and for the people," white Americans had condoned and accepted atrocious violence, on a mass scale, against vast numbers of dark-skinned fellow humans.

True, the original kidnapping and enslavement of Africans had been mostly the work of fellow Africans. But the treatment of the slaves as expendable commodities, and the gruesome packing and shipment of black bodies across the Atlantic, with calculated spoilage on the way, meant riches for white men, and New England shipowners as well as Southern slave traders had made fortunes in the business. Now, a hundred years after emancipation, the view that Negroes are an inferior race, prevailing in most of the North as well as the South, led to psychological if not physical violence against twenty million human beings. If ever, during three centuries of oppression, the oppressed threatened revolt, white America always had at its disposal the resources of violence known as law and order.

The National Association for the Advancement of Colored People had been engaged in legal battles against discrimination for over two generations. In close collaboration with white liberals, and working through legislation, court decisions, and a gradually sensitized public conscience, it had finally succeeded in eliminating the grosser forms of oppression. Lynching, which as late as the 1930's had occurred every few days somewhere in the South, had all but disappeared. To get the Supreme Court to ban Jim Crowism in the schools was a major breakthrough. "Freedom Now" and "We Shall Overcome" were the slogans of a new confidence.

Dr. Martin Luther King, Jr., had become the symbol and the prophet not only of the struggle for racial equality and justice but of the methods of non-violence and moral persuasion. The drama of his confrontations with police and courts, his mass demonstrations in hostile Southern cities, and finally the March on Washington in 1963, when he stirred tens of thousands of blacks and whites with his great "I have a dream" speech at the Lincoln Memorial—these were prodding the President and Congress into action.

A triumph of democratic social reform by peaceful means came with the passage of the civil right laws of 1964 and 1965. The efforts of SNCC and the volunteers from Northern colleges in those tense summer months of 1964 had resulted in only a few hundred Mississippi Negroes becoming voters, but the barriers had been broken, and within a few months of the 1965 Voting Rights Act half a million had been registered in five Deep South states. In a few more years a brother of murdered Medgar Evers would be elected mayor of a Mississippi town.

Yet for many these were shadowy triumphs. Northern Negroes had long had the vote, but in their ghettos "Freedom Now" meant little. In the South, ten years after the Supreme Court ruling, only two percent of the black children were in integrated schools. What good were laws if the "white power structure" which made them could flout them at its will?

A new and harsher mood was emerging. Blacks were asserting the right to lead the movement themselves. Younger and more militant leaders like James Forman, Stokely Carmichael, Floyd McKissick were taking over leadership of SNCC and CORE, and relegating their Ivy League and white liberal allies to menial tasks.

Non-violence was still accepted as a necessary method, because power was overwhelmingly on the other side. Non-violent confrontations with police had served to stir the conscience of white America, but to these new militants it was not a moral imperative. Even Dr. King had used the threat of others' violence as an instrument of persuasion. And if confrontations were likely to lead to violence anyway, were they not inviting it, even provoking it? Was the moral distinction so clear?

Like it or not, those who believed in gradual reform through the democratic process were having to face up to the fact that the whole civil rights movement seemed to have accepted the necessity of breaking the law. Black students sitting down in segregated lunchrooms and refusing to move to the back of buses, Dr. King leading banned demonstrations were lawbreakers. To be sure, federal courts declared the laws themselves illegal. And civil rights demonstrators were not the only lawbreakers. Southern governors had defied federal marshals seeking to carry out court orders. One had only to think back to the Prohibition era to realize that it was nothing new for Americans to feel that they could invoke their own ideas of freedom or justice against what they considered an intolerable law. But if there is no sanctity in constituted authority, in "law and order" as such, how stable is a social order?

The black revolt was raising increasingly uncomfortable questions for white America as it moved north. Public opinion of the white majority had tended to think of racial discrimination as a Southern problem. Most white city dwellers had been able to ignore the growth of black ghettos, except as their own neighborhoods were affected. They were suddenly shocked to full awareness in the mid 1960's when a new kind of violence flared. The Los Angeles ghetto, Watts, became a symbol of long suppressed black rage, which now burst into the open with cries of "Burn, baby, burn" and "Get Whitey." In four days and nights of August, 1965, thirty-five million dollars of damage was done in what had not even been considered a slum. Chicago and Cleveland suffered similar outbreaks the following summer, and in 1967 Newark, Detroit, and a dozen lesser cities were hit.

The chief targets of violence were buildings, usually white-owned shops and their contents. When the police and firemen tried to quell disorder and put out fires, they became targets for missiles, and even, on a few occasions, bullets. But the gutted blocks and the looted stores were in the ghetto themselves, and the chief sufferers were not "Whitey" but the local black residents whose neighborhoods were wrecked.

There had been race riots in the past in which blacks and whites had battled, but this was different. Sociologists, commissions of inquiry, and white liberals desperately sought for explanations.

The only comparable explosion in the American past had been the draft riots during the Civil War. Then it was disadvantaged immigrants, mostly Irish, in revolt against being drafted into a war they did not understand, going on a rampage of looting and burning that, before it was put down, left a thousand dead—more than in any of the new black ghetto disturbances. In both cases an oppressed minority was expressing its rage against established authority in undirected and insensate destruction.

At the very beginning of its investigations of the riots, the Kerner Commission disposed of the scapegoat explanation that they were inspired by communists or other conspirators. Nonetheless it recognized a revolutionary phenomenon.

The looters and the burners were predominantly young, but not necessarily of the most uneducated or deprived elements of the ghetto. While they knew they were defying accepted principles of private property and law and order, it was apparent that they felt justified in helping themselves, often with gleeful abandon, to the TV sets and luxuries of an affluent society which had rejected them.

Blocks of buildings burning out of control in the nation's capital might have been taken as a portent of the collapse of civilization, a reminder of the barbarians at the gates of Rome. But there was a strange quality of almost civilized restraint in the violence. The blacks were burning their own neighborhoods, not the homes of whites. Incidents of bodily violence against whites were rare. The violence had a symbolic quality. It was a kind of speech, of communication.

Few ghettos had a repeat performance. Little enough was done, to be sure, to meet the recommendations of the Kerner Commission, which called for massive commitments of money and good will to overcome the effect of what the commission blamed as "white racism." Yet in each case the ghetto had gone through a kind of internal purge. It was not only getting across its symbolic message, but the very spasm of self-destruction seemed a way of overcoming its sense of inferiority and helplessness. The young people who threw molotov cocktails might never become good citizens, but neither would they become what they felt so many of their elders had become: "Uncle Toms," docile victims of white supremacy.

Almost immediately a backlash began to make itself felt—not, as was feared, a white backlash so much as a reaction of the older residents of the ghetto, who realized that they were the chief victims.

A new slogan was now being heard: "Black is beautiful." The word "black" had been seized upon and transformed by black nationalist groups, of which the most successful in the early 1960's was the Nation of Islam, known as the Black Muslims. Malcolm X, their most dramatic spokesman until he broke with them and was assassinated in 1965, toured the nation's ghettos, lashing out at white racism, goading blacks to rise against the defeatist attitudes which still prevailed a hundred years after the Emancipation Proclamation had ended slavery as a legal institution. To him the word "Negro" was as much a white man's word as its Southern corruption into "Nigra" or "nigger." If people of the black race were to be emotionally freed from white domination they had to assert their blackness as a matter of pride.

A whole new generation of writers and artists had been making both whites and blacks in the literate public aware of the realities of the black soul, the "soul on ice," the "invisible man." Now in this mass movement of black self-assertion and black nationalism, millions of dark-skinned Americans faced white-skinned Americans for the first time without deference. They knew they were no longer "invisible."

For the black revolt, like the revolt of youth, was among other things a search for identity. A basic need of the individual human being is to feel identification with other human individuals, to feel that he belongs, that he is a part of some kind of social order. A human mind cannot keep its sanity as an isolated unit of consciousness in an infinite sea of nothingness. Even a slave had a sense of belonging, and where slavery involved direct human contact, as between a household slave and his owner, loyalty and even mutual respect were possible.

With the abolition of slavery at the end of the Civil War, the Negroes, uprooted and abandoned, were able to achieve some sense of security only by accepting an established position of inferiority. This worked after a fashion, as long as their labor was needed in the former slave states. But with the migration of Southern plantation workers to Northern cities, beginning at the time of the first World War, great numbers lost what little sense of identity they had had in a white man's world. Domestic service, mostly for women, tended to leave the men with no function, and stable family life was difficult to achieve in the ghetto jungles. The damage could not be undone without a new assertion of the Negro as a person, a black person, a person in his own right.

The Negro revolt was thus related to the moral revolt of young people generally, feeling themselves strangers in an alien land, asserting the right to be recognized as persons. It also owed more than it wished to acknowledge to the humanistic, democratic tradition, which was based on the premise that all men are endowed with certain inalienable rights, and had finally begun to give blacks the chance to assert those rights.

That the blacks had now seized the initiative was clearly seen in what happened as the campuses of Northern colleges and universities opened their gates to black students. Northern college administrators who had sought them out were shocked and hurt, and well-meaning white students had their advances rebuffed, when black students began awakening to the new sense of their own value. Afro hair-dos and dress, demands for "black studies," even for separatism, flying in the face of the drive against segregation, all testified to the mood of a new generation which no longer wanted to be integrated, or to be called by the polite white word "Negro," but preferred the once despised "black."

With the new sense of personal significance came a new assertiveness, a new militancy symbolized by the slogan "black power."

When Stokely Carmichael took over the leadership of the Student Nonviolent Coordinating Committee in 1965, and demanded "black power," a shiver of apprehension went through much of white America and shook the older civil rights movement. Was this a call for violent revolution?

The young black militants like Carmichael were themselves not sure. The phrase obviously had appeal to many who believed in neither violence nor revolution. Some liberal reformers could accept it as an expression of a legitimate claim to share in running the affairs of the country along with its many other minorities, but most of them realized that it was more than that. The new pride of race which had expressed itself in the phrase "black is beautiful" was no longer willing to think of the goal as simple acceptance into a white man's world.

The civil rights movement had up until then been dominated by the idea of acceptance, the elimination of discrimination based on skin color. It is true that some of the early black nationalists had called for a return to Africa, and that Marcus Garvey had proclaimed the "African Republic" at a gathering in New York fifty years before. They had insisted that there was no future for the Negro as a minority within the white man's world. But neither a return to Africa, nor a Negro enclave within the United States, nor "self-determination for the Black Belt," which the Communists made a campaign slogan in the early 1930's, offered a practical solution, and the mixture of pragmatism and idealism in the National Association for the Advancement of Colored People had remained the measure of Negro hopes. Now, as its long and bloody battle against segregation and discrimination seemed on the point of victory, why the new emphasis on black separateness?

Why, if the Negro wins equal opportunity in education and employment, can he not be integrated into American society? Other minority groups—German, Irish, Jewish, Italian, Polish—in successive waves of immigrants, had fought exclusion and discrimination and finally achieved full participation in American life.

To the white American his own experience seemed encouraging. Here the better part of a continent had been living under one governmental system for a period of almost unprecedented length, with only one major violent struggle for power in almost two hundred years. It had proclaimed the supremacy of the moral law. Its motto was unity in diversity, and it boasted of being a melting pot. Even its exclusionary immigration policy which, first by historical accident and then by law, had put a premium on North European origin, was, at least in principle, now repudiated.

But those whose forefathers had been shipped as slaves saw America differently. They had not been assimilated. Even the racial mixing that had occurred everywhere, as an incident of white mastery over black slaves, had merely extended the badge of blackness to a variety of browns and yellows.

Skin color made the difference. The darker the color, the more the difference. Few red-skinned Indians, or Mexicans, or Puerto Ricans, with varying shades of brown, or Asians (except perhaps in Hawaii) had yet won complete assimilation. The blacks had it worst, thanks to slavery. No white man was wholly untainted by the inherited attitudes of the master. No black could wholly escape his own cruel heritage.

Negroes might accept Puerto Ricans as allies, for many of them were descendants of black slaves, and they were now neighbors in the ghettos of the big cities. But they felt no common interest with other non-white minorities. Their own special heritage set them apart. No matter how light their color, how mixed their ancestry, unless they had chosen to pass as whites—as some, hiding their "Negro blood," had been able to do over the years—they were now blacks. They were different. They were separate. They were the victims of those who had the power.

Their most charismatic leaders were telling them that never in the history of man on the planet had there been such cruelty and injustice inflicted on any people as by whites against blacks. Yet history is replete with conquests and slaughters and enslavements. In the violent struggle of ethnic groups, the powerful have survived and have written their own history. What black students were now reading was white man's history, yet even there it was possible to see his predatory character. Whether the white race was genetically more violent and aggressive than other races, there was no doubt that in the modern era white peoples had conquered or dominated most of the world, and power was what counted.

In any case, when young blacks now responded to the call for black power, they were, consciously or not, following in the wake of innumerable ethnic groups in the long history of man who have sought to shake off oppression and to seek their own place in the sun on their own terms.

Yet this history left them with hard questions to answer. How, after all, do the oppressed free themselves from oppression?

In earlier times they might have escaped to new land, or taken the land of others weaker than themselves. Moses was a symbol of the leader who liberated a people from slavery and led them to a promised land, formerly theirs, which they then reconquered. But for the blacks the return to Africa was now not even a romantic dream. And there was no new land. The days of homesteading in America had passed. The settlers who had filled the land, often themselves minorities in flight from oppression, were certainly not going to let blacks establish their own country, or even their own state within the United States.

Freed from slavery, in a country whose official creed was the equality of men and whose Constitution gave official protection to the rights of petition and assembly, it had taken the Negroes a hundred years to win anything like full implementation, on the statute books and in the courts, of rights which white Anglo-Saxon Protestants had enjoyed since Magna Carta. Yet "freedom now" had not been realized. Was American democracy after all a delusion? Was it, now and forever, for whites only? Or could blacks ultimately gain at least their rightful share of power?

People of different ages naturally gave different answers.

The traditional civil rights movement pointed to the power already achieved through the ballot, with black mayors elected in cities and towns, even in the Deep South. White liberals, prompted by conscience as well as the instinct for survival, had been pushing vast social welfare programs, community action in a thousand communities, model cities to replace gutted slums: with a massively financed war on poverty, might the Negro achieve continuing democratic progress, if not a great society? Statistics of rising employment and rising incomes, and the growing number of well-to-do black business and professional men lent encouragement to believers in "black capitalism," which might lead painlessly, if slowly, into general affluence.

But these are all distant hopes. The young are impatient, and are seeking their own answers. Some have accepted the Black Panthers' belief that blacks can be liberated only by violent revolution to overthrow what they see as an all-encompassing system of colonial oppression and capitalist exploitation. The Panthers have been arming themselves for the street battles which their own talk of guerrilla warfare has made more probable. Though the Black Panthers number at most only a few thousand, their attitude is affecting many other young people.

Now winning admission in growing volume to previously all-white colleges, black students are finding college life to be very different from that of a generation ago. Campuses are now riven by the cultural revolution, the new "life style," the moral revolt of white youth against the Vietnam war.

Black militants who are ready to push civil disobedience on to rebellion, protest into guerrilla war, and revolt into revolution find on the campuses and in the intellectual circles they are now entering that other young people are already talking revolution. Whether or not it is the same revolution, black students and white students find themselves confronting the same university establishments. When the police are called, law and order looks the same to both. Some, at least, of the militant blacks realize that black power can be achieved only in alliance with others seeking power. Perhaps the campus is the place to start.

3 | Campus Revolt

The revolt that swept American campuses in the latter part of the 1960's was certainly not planned. It was not even foreseen, though in retrospect perhaps it should have been.

Its origins had little to do with the traditional concerns of college and university. Never had so many had so much: more young people were able to secure higher education, of better quality, in a freer atmosphere, than was ever dreamed of before in history. Here was no uprising of a poor and oppressed class driven to desperation by tyranny, though many students felt abused and downtrodden. Rather it was a phase of the more general cultural and moral revolt of the young.

It began with the drop-outs. They had no thought of challenging the mighty porticos and ivy-covered walls. They simply left. Many bright boys and girls could not see the sense of enduring four to ten years of an academic grind just to get into the "rat race" in which they saw their parents trapped. Yet many of them hung around the outskirts of college communities. Perhaps they merely wanted to be near their contemporaries; or perhaps, hungry for knowledge and understanding, they felt that within the academic walls there must be some answers to the riddle of existence. They took up cults and causes which gave them a sense of belonging to something significant. Around the campus of the University of California at Berkeley they were called "street people," and consciously or unconsciously they prodded student rebels into the first overt action.

Two non-academic causes were particularly disturbing to the traditional ivory-tower atmosphere at institutions like Berkeley. One, of course, was the war in Vietnam. Many students, hating the hypocrisies and atrocities of the war and the universities' involvement in the war, came to hate almost as much the web of credits and academic irrelevancies which were their only protection from the draft. At the same time, the vast churning of the American conscience over the racial discrimination that had so long been taken for granted was particularly affecting a new generation of students. The emotional fervor of the peace movement and the new protest techniques of the civil rights movement suddenly erupted on the American campus.

The Berkeley uprisings began in 1964 on the issue of free speech, when the university administration tried to move what it considered outside agitators off the campus. The traditional arbitrariness of the making and enforcing of rules on college and university campuses suddenly struck students who had never before seriously questioned the system. One student leader, Mario Savio, who had spent the previous long hot summer in Mississippi as a civil rights volunteer, effectively applied his experience of civil disobedience and confrontation at the university.

The Freedom Ride and the sit-in were the precursors of the seizure of an administration building. When the police were called and used force to clear out the protesters, the university appeared for the first time to many students as a part of a despotic system of which they were the victims.

Revolution on the campus became a spectacular, live on TV, which helped to spread the revolt from campus to campus, and the alarm from one center of the Establishment to another. In 1968 the student revolt exploded at Columbia University. By that time the black revolt was flaring in the ghetto, and black students were demanding academic programs that would not leave them mere imitations of white intellectuals. By that time, too, the inability of the country either to win the war in Vietnam or to extricate itself was a source of maddening frustration.

Yet both the race issue and the war issue were peripheral at Columbia. When buildings were seized in the effort to enforce student demands, black students who had taken Hamilton Hall kept out not only professors but white radicals, as if to say their revolt was quite different from that of the white students. And when student leaders sought for issues linking the university with the war in Vietnam, they readily found them in R.O.T.C., war research, and recruitment by arms manufacturers. But what these issues, like the free speech issue at Berkeley, had finally revealed as the basic grievance was the lack of democracy in the university, and in the social order to which it now seemed to hold the key.

The basic fact was that colleges and universities, in the United States as in the rest of the world, had somehow escaped the democratic revolutions that had swept the world since 1776. Legally the American college or university is organized like a business corporation; it is under the ostensible direction of trustees whose main interests are elsewhere, and under the actual authority of administrative officers and faculties. The administration has had virtually absolute authority in matters of business and financial management, and in the admission and control of students. Faculties have determined what is taught and have controlled the recruitment and advancement of their own personnel. As communities of scholars in often unrelated departments of knowledge, they have tended to think of their students as transient customers to whom they had to give part of their time, or as indentured apprentices to whom they passed on their special skills during a period of disciplined tutelage.

Generations of students had docilely accepted this conception of institutions of higher learning as privileged enclaves to which they were briefly admitted as outsiders, and where they might be allowed to remain as long as they obeyed the rules. They might feel attached to an alma mater, as children to their mother, and traditionally they loyally supported the football team. Student councils and student government were encouraged, to be sure, but more as a part of a training in good citizenship than as means for responsible participation in the university as a democratic enterprise.

When the phrase "student power" was first heard at a National Student Association convention in 1965 it aroused almost as much consternation in the Establishment as the phrase "black power" which had prompted it. The NSA had been the respectable trade association of respectable student councils and, as was discovered about this time, it had for a few years been secretly subsidized by the Central Intelligence Agency as a safe counterweight to the supposed threat of communist infiltration. Now it was becoming a spearhead of the revolt of the young. It was infiltrated not by foreign ideologies, though some student radicals had begun learning about revolutions of other times and places, but by the more militant of the youthful rebels who were finding the assumptions of American democracy belied by racial discrimination, military adventures, and the false values of a consumer culture.

The Students for a Democratic Society began to attract some of the boldest and most idealistic of the new generation of students. At its organizing convention at Port Huron, Michigan, in 1962, the S.D.S. had issued a manifesto which laid out its accusations against a racist and militarist America, and raised the new ideal of "participatory democracy."

The positive appeal of that slogan was obscured, and the more immediately relevant demand for student power was distorted, often beyond recognition, by the growing vogue for obscenity and deliberately outrageous behavior. The free speech movement at Berkeley had been followed up, half in jest, to be sure, and mostly by "street people," with the "filthy speech movement." Some campus radicals —already offensive to both university and civil authorities, to solid citizens and the police, by reason of their long hair, dirty levis, and general derelict appearance—seemed to want to test the limits of tolerance with their insults and gutter words, as they pushed professors out of buildings, seized microphones at public meetings, and engaged in occasional wanton acts of vandalism.

When the police were called in by frightened administrators, they were greeted with epithets which up until that time had been considered so unprintable as to require a row of asterisks. At Columbia and other universities, as later at the Chicago Democratic Convention, the police reacted with violence.

Contrary to the impression created by some of the news media, student violence has most often been only the symbolic violence of word and gesture. One survey of protests on 232 campuses found that in 76 percent there had been no violence or destruction of any kind. Most students, even if they did not participate, tended to sympathize with the protests and blamed university authorities and the police for violence when it did occur. Only one faction of the splintering S.D.S., the Weathermen, openly espoused street fighting and vandalism, and its influence on campuses was never great.

Some campus violence is perhaps attributable to simple immaturity. Children like to shout forbidden bathroom words. Spring riots and panty raids have been hallowed college traditions. More to the point, infantile rage, real or make-believe, often finds release in vandalism, breaking windows, smashing the more vulnerable artifacts of the grown-up world. Destructive drives under civilized and adult exteriors were recognized long before Freud. Moreover, individual circumstances can warp and twist human nature into ugly shapes, which emerge, not surprisingly, in times of tension and unrest. Finally, if the more sinister and sadistic of man's proclivities are usually repressed, nothing releases them more readily than the mood of a mob with a sense of righteous indignation.

Yet more valid justifications can be offered for the apparent barbarity of some student protests. A movement which is conceived as one of liberation from the prevailing hypocrisies of our times, as well as from its oppressions, has made a virtue of freedom in its use of words and in its manners. The outlandishness of the new "life style" may seem to an older generation as rigidly conformist as the gray-flannel suits of a few years ago, but still it is a declaration of independence. To the student activists, of course, no such explanations are needed. In their eyes, all the violence originates with the police and the university administrators who call in the police to suppress legiti-

mate student protests. If students throw rocks or occasionally vandal-
ize university buildings, these are only natural reactions, say their
apologists, to the brutalities and injustices inflicted on them.

The seizure of a building has often seemed to students, with considerable justification, to be the only means by which they could induce
university administrators to listen to their grievances. Such a seizure,
however unconventional or illegal, is, in their view, a non-violent form
of civil disobedience, and if violence is used by police to remove them
this only confirms their conviction that ours is a social order of oppression maintained by naked force. To those who have concluded that the
needed radical changes cannot be won without violence, any stimulus
to violence is justifiable, but this view is still that of only a very small
minority.

The great majority of restless students today are not naturally ad-
dicted to violence. Nor are they under the influence of any particular
social or political ideology. Even the political issues that have stirred
them in this country are not the root causes they seem, for students
in other countries with different issues are rebelling in the same way.
Nor is the revolt limited to college students confronting university
authorities. The American high school also is now a battleground.

The changes in appearance and behavior which have been the
outward mark of the revolt of the young, from superficialities such as
length of hair to the use of dangerous drugs, have affected children
even in primary schools. Rebellion against long accepted patterns of
school discipline, whether justified or not, finds sanction in a society
which for fifty years has been shifting away from the tradition of strict
parental authority toward extreme permissiveness.

At what point should a child make decisions for himself? The
question first arises in earliest infancy, when a mother chooses either
to feed her baby whenever he cries, or to follow a pediatrician's
schedule of feedings. The conflict between the desire of the human
individual to be free and the demands of the society to which it must
conform to survive is present in all societies and at all times.

In primitive societies, as in the most advanced, the anthropologist
finds the elders—chiefs, headmen, kings or chief executives—requir-

ing the young to conform to the patterns of social behavior that have proved to have survival value. Our own legal system, which can trace its origins directly back to pre-agricultural patterns and has many attitudes derived from ancient Rome and medieval Europe, still considers a person an "infant," without power to make a binding contract, until the age of twenty-one. A husband and father had almost absolute rights of ownership over his children and womenfolk until the liberating democratic ideas of the French and American revolutions. Even today, the emotionally warped or distraught parent who is brought into court in a so-called battered child case is likely to betray inherited attitudes that a child is a possession rather than a person.

Humane and enlightened concern by society has in the last hundred years enacted protective legislation—child labor laws, juvenile court procedures and the like—which has recognized that children, too, are persons, with the same inalienable rights to life, liberty, and the pursuit of happiness as adults. At the same time the democratic ethic has been extended to the home and family and school. The more conservative elders now think we have gone too far. A few years ago they were complaining that with the granting of equal rights to women ours had become a matriarchal society, dominated by "Mom" if not yet by a "Madam President." Now they are saying it is a child-dominated society, in which parents are terrorized by their free-wheeling children. In some respects the charge is perhaps justified. Yet there is no doubt that the basic decisions of society are still made by adult males. Despite the changes of the last fifty years, it is still a society in which children are told what to do. But what is a "child"? When does childhood end? When is a person competent to be on his own?

In earlier times, when the cultural heritage was briefer and simpler, children became adult members of the tribe at puberty. While physical maturity now comes at an earlier age, thanks to better nutrition and health care, the accumulating cultural heritage and the specialization of knowledge and skills have stretched out the dependent periods of childhood and youth, until sometimes a young person entering a profession is not self-supporting until the mid-thirties. Yet, for all the delay in achieving economic independence, an eighth-grader is likely to be vastly better educated than the most learned of his ancestors a few generations ago.

The spread of the democratic idea and the increase in sophistication with universal education now reinforce the demands of young people to be treated as people. They recognize no point on the age scale at which the right to determine their own destiny begins. They are only too well aware of the limitations of their own competence, but they want to be taken seriously.

All over the country, but chiefly in the big cities where the influx of blacks from the South and the flight of whites to the suburbs have suddenly raised appallingly difficult problems of adjustment, school systems have been subjected to excruciating strains. School administrators, long accustomed to ruling their domains within long established patterns of discipline and bureaucratic certainty, have been challenged from every side: by the courts requiring desegregation, by striking teachers, by black parents stirred by ghetto confrontations, by white parents whose children are now paying the price of past prejudice, and most of all by young people in revolt against all authority, no longer afraid of imposed discipline but having learned little self-discipline.

In both high schools and colleges, revolt is likely to show itself first with respect to rules of decorum rather than over academic or social issues. Since outward appearance has such symbolic importance in the whole youth rebellion, it is naturally a touchy issue for a school principal or a college dean to deal with. Ordering a boy with shoulder-length hair to cut it can cast the wielder of authority in the role of cruel despot, and spark a rebellion.

Traditionally, and as a matter of law, the teacher has stood *in loco parentis*. He was held responsible for imparting good morals as well as knowledge. When education beyond the primary level could be obtained only at a boarding academy or a residential college, away from home, rules of behavior were laid down, often in quite intimate detail, including matters of dress, manners, neatness, cleanliness, punctuality, and, most certainly, sex. Some of these regulations, often called parietal or house rules, were needed for the orderly operation of any group activity. Others were justifiable in terms of training in the disciplines needed for responsible citizenship.

As the education explosion of the last fifty years has opened not only secondary education but at least two years of post-secondary education to all, the traditional role of the schoolmaster as substitute parent has become difficult if not impossible to maintain. With changing styles of dress and personal grooming, and abandonment of strict discipline in the home in favor of freedom of expression, inherited rules of old-fashioned decorum came to seem increasingly irksome. Restrictions on sexual freedom and on the use of drugs further alienated the student generation from campus father figures.

Yet the campus revolt was far more than a revolt against rules of behavior that had lost their legitimacy in the eyes of the young. The slogan "student power," like the slogan "black power" from which it was derived, went beyond resentment at being pushed around. It was a demand to be treated not merely as a person with rights, but as an active citizen. It was a demand for a share in making decisions, for participation in governing the educational communities of which they were members, for a voice in their country's policies.

One of the complaints against the draft was that if young men were old enough to be called upon to fight for their country, they should be considered old enough to vote. With the spread of the idea of democracy in the last two hundred years has come the demand of one large category of persons after another for an effective voice in government, and each such demand has been met by the horrified resistance of those already qualified to rule. When monarchy and hereditary privilege gave way to republican and representative institutions, it was assumed that only men of property could be trusted to vote. As the pressure for universal manhood suffrage increased, the men of property raised the question of how people without the qualities of mind and character needed to acquire and keep personal wealth could presume to share in governing the commonwealth. To answer them, it was not necessary to claim that all men are competent to govern, only that men of property are incompetent to govern other than in their own interest.

When women dared to claim equal rights and finally to demand the vote itself, many males resisted with the same appeal to competence: How could women, whose place was with their children and in the kitchen, deal with man's public affairs? Again the question of competence was legitimate, but could equally well be turned against husbands' making rules for their wives. When industrial workers sought to protect their interests through unions, and even sought political power through labor lobbies or labor parties, the specialists in business and finance and government felt the working man's intrusion to be both dangerous and absurd.

So now, when university students, often with intolerable rudeness, demand a share in running a university community, middle-aged trustees and administrators and professors ask incredulously, what competence have they?

What can an entering freshman know about a university budget? Even after four undergraduate years, can a senior vote responsibly on the recruitment of faculty, or the setting up of new departments? On the other hand, one may equally well ask what a newly made voter can understand of the intricate issues of national and international politics which may be affected by his vote on election day.

In any case, and regardless of competence, the democratic tide, here as in other areas, is irresistible. It is no longer a question of the legitimacy of student power, but of where and how much.

The most spectacular campus confrontations have, however, often seemed to be less concerned with student participation in academic decisions than with the urgent issues of race, urban decay, and the war in Vietnam.

The connection between the race issue and university policy has usually been clear. When black students have been involved in campus confrontations they were demanding "black studies," or increased enrollment of black students and faculty, or special recognition and facilities for black students.

Urban problems have frequently been raised by white student radicals as a means of turning discontent with archaic university structures and attitudes into social protest. At Columbia, for instance, the building of a new gymnasium in a public park at the edge of the ghetto was denounced, not too convincingly, as callous racism, and the university's plans for new buildings at the expense of evicted slum dwellers was made to seem calculated oppression. Berkeley students helped turn a vacant lot into a "people's park," and then resisted tear gas and shotguns when the University of California asserted its rights of ownership. Whenever universities have called in police to prevent destruction and disruption by students, this has been resented as a violation of the special academic sanctuary of the campus and has tended to unite moderates and radicals in protest.

Even if the relations of the university to the local community have sometimes been given spurious emphasis by radical leaders as a means of radicalizing the rest of the student body, the issue remains a valid one. Universities will never again be able to isolate themselves from the problems of their urban neighbors. And on community-related issues students may have a special claim to be involved in university decisions, for they often live in the neighborhoods affected. On such issues they may have not less but more competence than university trustees or administrators or even faculty members.

In yet another area of university policy, the ties of the university to the war in Vietnam and the arms race, students feel they have an even more intimate concern, justifying their demand for a voice. They know they will be doing the fighting if war continues to be the preoccupation of society; they will be doing the dying if the university continues as the docile servant of a military-industrial corporate state. Competent or not, they are not outsiders.

If any still thought they were, the illusion vanished in the spring of 1970 when the bullets of law and order killed four white students at Kent State University in Ohio and two black ones at Jackson State in Mississippi in the course of protests related to the expansion of the Vietnam war into Cambodia.

The campus revolt is, in fact, inseparable from the revolt against war.

4 | Revolt Against War

Concern with mounting violence became acute toward the end of the 1960's. Paradoxically, much of the violence was in protest against violence. The increasing turbulence of the civil rights movement stemmed from violent indignities long suffered. Campus radicalism was rooted in revulsion against the war in Vietnam. The aims of even the most violent of the rebels were peace and brotherhood.

But there was neither peace nor brotherhood in what Americans saw on their TV screens in 1968. Many were coming to the conclusion that American democracy was being overwhelmed.

The murder of Martin Luther King, the chief apostle of non-violence, proved to militant blacks that non-violence could never succeed, and the wave of ghetto riots that followed reached almost to the steps of the White House. The assassination of Robert Kennedy shortly thereafter intensified the feeling of many young white radicals that social change could not be achieved by conventional political methods, and gave new emphasis to their talk of revolution. Universities and research foundations as well as presidential commissions began to undertake studies of violence as a grave social phenomenon.

Then in late summer came the climactic events in Chicago at the time of the Democratic National Convention. TV viewers saw convention delegates and newsmen manhandled by security guards on the convention floor. They saw marching mobs of uncouth young people attacked by club-swinging police.

Again most of the violence was perpetrated in the name of peace. The police were ostensibly maintaining domestic peace. The taunts and obscenities which, with a few more solid missiles, roused some of them to fury, were flung by young people demanding peace in Vietnam. The assembly of the thousands of demonstrators, which led to the massive police action, was in fact a climax of a mounting peace movement.

One of the dramatic contrasts brought out by the cameramen, both at the time of the riots and in the conspiracy trial in the following year, was between the older pacifists and the new, between the chairman of the organizing committee for the protest demonstrations, David Dellinger, clean-shaven and in business suit and tie, and the leaders of the Yippies, hirsute Jerry Rubin and Abbie Hoffman. Dellinger represented the traditional religious and philosophical rejection of war as mass murder, scientifically and rationally indefensible. He believed in non-violence both as a means and as an end. Though he found himself at the head of what seemed to Mayor Daley and his police a revolutionary mob, he was essentially a reformer.

Rubin and Hoffman, on the other hand, were spokesmen for an extreme element in the cultural revolt which condemned our civilization for being too scientific and rational. They and their picturesque followers not only believed in a future revolution to release spontaneity of feeling and expression, but also believed that by living as if the revolution were here and now they could help make it so.

Between these extremes were leaders of the campus revolt like Tom Hayden, a founder of the Students for a Democratic Society, who combined a liberal idealism with the toughness of a professional revolutionist. When the federal government later undertook to prosecute the leaders of the Chicago mobilization as a criminal conspiracy, the Black Panther leader Bobby Seale was included, though, as every TV viewer had observed, virtually all the participants in the demonstrations had been white.

While David Dellinger represented a traditional pacifist movement which had been gathering strength for generations, he was also a product of two new elements in the peace movement. One derived from Hiroshima, the other from Gandhi.

The first atom bomb had convinced many that war was now not just immoral but insane. As the two most powerful nations began to amass thousands of weapons, each thousands of times as powerful as the Hiroshima bomb, and the fate of nations, if not of the human race itself, seemed to hang on a balance of doomsday machines labeled "security," pacifism acquired a powerful new appeal. The National Committee for a Sane Nuclear Policy appropriately emphasized the word SANE, and kept insisting that it was madness to think that peace could depend on the ultimate in violence.

At the same time, a new mode for expression of moral outrage was being developed. It first made headlines in 1960 when members of a newly formed Committee for Non-Violent Action engaged in acts of civil disobedience to protest the launching of submarines designed to carry nuclear weapons. Some risked their lives by invading the launching area, at Groton, Connecticut, in small boats, or swam to interpose bare flesh in symbolic protest against the monsters of annihilation. Others pushed their way into the private property of the General Dynamics Corporation shipyard, as they had into various military and naval installations around the country, courting arrest and imprisonment to dramatize their protest. This was not civil disobedience of unconstitutional or immoral laws, but was simple trespass, or violation of harbor regulations, where the authority challenged was engaged in what was felt to be an immoral policy.

In this the challengers were following the moral and political example of Gandhi. In his famous Salt March to the sea, he had singled out the government monopoly of salt production as a symbol of the subjection of India to the British Empire; the simple gesture of scooping up sea water to make salt illegally helped bring the British Empire tumbling down.

The leader of the Committee for Non-Violent Action was a former Protestant minister, A. J. Muste, revered by many as the American Gandhi. He was then nearing eighty, but his followers were mostly recruits from the revolt of youth, some in their teens. To solid citizens their protests seemed childish antics, and when they appeared at the shipyard, long-haired and possibly barefoot, carrying their banners, they were put down as relatively harmless beatniks, no more than minor irritants. Even liberals of an earlier generation, who deplored nuclear weapons and the war in Vietnam, felt that the Gandhian style was unlikely to convert anyone. The extremes to which the protesters carried non-violence in going limp when arrested, so as not to cooperate with what they considered an evil system of authority, or in refusing to stand in a courtroom before a judge because to them he represented an unjust legal system, sometimes led older sympathizers to feel that psychiatric help was more in order than punishment.

Yet there was no doubt that these sometimes bizarre acts of symbolic protest stirred the consciences of the cautious and conventional, and contributed to the growing revulsion against the war in Vietnam. At times these young pacifists seemed fanatical and even offensively arrogant in their confident pose of moral superiority. They fasted and they prayed, but they were also willing to risk life and liberty for their beliefs. They staged exhausting vigils outside military posts in protest against new and more fiendish weapons. They entered forbidden areas, inviting arrest and sometimes serving long terms in federal prisons. They trudged hundreds and thousands of miles in protest marches, trying to break through the smug acceptance of evil by their fellow men. When they were derided for not protesting the arms race to the Russians too, they organized a six-month march from San Francisco to Moscow. Facing apathy and hostility on both sides of the Atlantic and on both sides of the Iron Curtain, they were finally hustled under police surveillance to be formally greeted by the Kremlin's official peace spokesmen.

Their dedicated witness to our universal humanity and the highest values of our religious heritage gave not only the peace movement, but also the whole revolt of their generation a moral emphasis that only added to the discomfort of their elders.

Among the pacifists were young women and others not subject to the draft or exempted from service, and many who might have won exemption but chose rather to oppose the whole military system. Yet for them, as indeed for the whole generation coming of age during the 1960's, the draft was a major concern. Hundreds of thousands were influenced by the pacifist movement, and derived from it a moral and intellectual support for their growing rebellion. What for many may have started as mere antipathy to military discipline and the discomforts and hazards of military life in steaming jungles on the other side of the world, became indignation at being conscripted for the cruel business of killing and being killed and ended up as revolt against the policies and politics and politicians that had forced this horror upon them.

Their elders, and particularly those making the often hard decisions to escalate the war in Vietnam, could not readily understand or sympathize with this rebellion of the young. In no area was the generation gap more apparent. Yet not only did it set the son against the father, but the inner lesion often set each against himself. Even the conscientious objector could rarely be sure that his motives included no element of fear, or of the desire of the pampered child to avoid the rigors and the dangers of the soldier's life.

The military virtues are enshrined in tradition. A Roman poet wrote that "it is sweet and fitting to die for one's country." Under feudalism the armored knight became the epitome of manhood and nobility of character. Even as late as the first World War young men volunteered to fight as if for high adventure. For many survivors of both World Wars, the sense of common effort in a great cause was a cherished memory, outweighing any horrors endured. Without doubt, many veterans think of their war service as the best years of their lives.

Nobody any longer thinks of war as fun, but most young Americans, indoctrinated with love of country and reared in the traditional attitudes, began by accepting the draft, and even combat service in Vietnam, as natural and unavoidable. Yet the spreading cultural and moral revolt of the young, and the mounting skepticism at all age levels about the Vietnam adventure, nourished the growing resistance to the draft.

There were, of course, legitimate grounds for exemption, but these

added to the tensions, rather than allaying them. Educational defer-
ments, which lured many to go on to college and postgraduate work,
only contributed to the campus restlessness of those who had no other
reason to prolong their days in school. The draft law allowed exemption for those who, because of religious training and belief, came
within the legal definition of conscientious objectors; however, the
attitudes of the rebellious young did not fit conventional notions of
religious belief, and this offered a way out for relatively few. Many
young people simply agreed with a growing number of their elders
that the war in Vietnam was morally unjustifiable, and, without taking
the absolutist position of the religious pacifist against all war, they
were against this war and wanted no part of it.

Whatever the reasons for the prospective draftee's objections, once
he had decided to resist the draft he still had to choose between
alternatives. He could refuse to register on reaching the age of eigh-
teen, but few did so. Most accepted their draft cards and hoped for
the best before ultimate induction. It was when notified to appear for
induction that the objector usually faced his agonizing decision. Unless he was a member of a group, and felt supported by the group, he
might accept his fate. But thousands did not. Many waited to be
arrested, and accepted long prison terms with courage. Many more
took to the road, hoping the law would not catch up with them. Many
fled the country, particularly to Canada, which, after some hesitation,
decided to let them stay.

Still others, having been drafted and in some cases shipped overseas,
deserted, and the draft evaders were joined in their shifting and inse-
cure refuges by those who had left their uniforms behind.

Avoidance of military service was not new in America. The Civil
War had seen bloody rioting against the draft. Americans had refused
to fight in two world wars, and in the Korean War of the 1950's there
had been thousands of deserters. But in the 1960's it was different.
Rebellion against other aspects of American society was rampant.
Organizations were available so that the draft resister need not resist
alone.

Some of the organized effort went into providing legal advice and

more general counseling on how to avoid the draft. A kind of underground railroad, reminiscent of the network that developed to assist
escaping slaves a hundred years ago, facilitated escape of draft evaders
and deserters to Canada. Moral and financial support came from some
peace organizations which had long been operating openly and legally.

Many older Americans, whether moved by humanitarian principles
or religious conviction, or simply disagreement with American foreign
policy, had to wrestle with the same kind of painful decisions as their
sons. Was civil disobedience—lawbreaking—legitimate in opposing
the war in Vietnam? They might have contributed to organizations
like SANE or the Fellowship of Reconciliation, and then have felt that
all the efforts of publicity, protest meetings, lobbying in Washington,
letters to the editor, and even peaceful marches and demonstrations
had had no apparent effect in changing the country's course. Civil
disobedience had helped in the fight against discrimination. It might
help stop the war.

Young demonstrators had begun burning draft cards. Though only
a symbolic protest, it carried severe criminal penalties. Hundreds gave
up their draft cards to be collected and turned in at draft board offices
or induction centers. Girls and middle-aged women, priests and
professors, joined draft resisters in breaking into draft offices, pouring
pig's blood on draft records or looting files and scattering their shred-
ded contents in street demonstrations. Such activities were clearly
punishable as crimes. But the limits of legal protest were not easy to
define. Dr. Benjamin Spock, Yale Chaplain William Sloane Coffin, Jr.,
and others who encouraged the draft resisters, were tried and convicted on charges of conspiracy to aid and abet interference with the
draft, but their conviction was reversed on appeal.

Even within the armed forces, along with individual desertions and
refusals to obey particular orders on grounds of conscience, a more
general unrest was growing. An underground press began publishing
anti-war propaganda and grievances against military life, at military
camps and even in Vietnam. Coffeehouses at camp gates provided
meeting grounds for the disaffected. When military authorities took
steps to ban publications or coffeehouses, liberal organizations

brought legal action in the name of free speech and assembly. In the summer of 1969 the Defense Department gave reluctant recognition to dissent, where it involved no direct incitements to criminal or mutinous action. Yet clearly dissent by men in uniform was a disturbing development. Revolutions begin with mutiny in the armed forces. Army commanders were jittery. When a few prisoners in a San Francisco military stockade joined in a brief sit-down protest against the killing of a prisoner by a guard, they were convicted of mutiny and sentenced to up to fifteen years' imprisonment. A nationwide protest later achieved partial mitigation of those sentences. Eventually came a report from South Vietnam that a company of soldiers, battle-weary beyond endurance, had refused an order to advance. The mutiny lasted only a few hours, and the Army made light of it, but it was still mutiny.

Still there was little ground to believe that the armed forces generally were seriously disaffected. Revolt against the war, though initiated and inspired by the older liberal movement and by religious pacifism, was still primarily an aspect of the general revolt of youth. It was both symptom and cause of the campus revolt. Its relation to the black revolt was not quite so direct, though Dr. Martin Luther King and many others had tried to link that movement to the struggle of the dark-skinned Vietnamese against white domination, and almost all the civil rights groups took a strong stand against the war.

The methods used by the peace movement, also, were the same as those used in the civil rights struggle. Within the accepted limits of what was legal, both movements made full use of meetings, publicity, advertisements, letters to the editor, and demonstrations, to influence public opinion and change governmental policies. But a growing segment of the peace movement, particularly the draft resisters, were prepared to go beyond the limits of legality. As in the civil rights movement and in the campus revolt, they were engaging in symbolic civil disobedience as a form of protest and as a means of getting public attention. For the most part, this civil disobedience was peaceful and non-violent, in conformity with its ultimate goals. But, again under the influence of the young, and the growing radicalization on the campus and in the civil rights struggle, and even more when demonstrators felt police violence loosed against them in the name of law and order, they were inclined to abandon non-violence even as a tactic. The revolt against war, like the civil rights movement and the campus revolt, was becoming revolutionary in its talk, and perhaps in its implications.

The older peace movements appealed to humanitarianism and one-world idealism; they sought by influencing public opinion to induce governments to renounce war and create new international machinery to enforce peace. They envisaged a world government evolving from a strengthened United Nations. Their enemies were ignorance and inherited prejudice and the stubbornness of past loyalties.

To those pacifists who were motivated chiefly by religious and moral concerns, the enemy was essentially the evil in man or in his institutions or both, evil which hopefully might be overcome by love and sacrifice.

But neither the peace movements nor the pacifists set the tone for the growing disillusionment with the war in Vietnam, as it reached mass proportions in the late 1960's. This was a revulsion of the nation's conscience against a mounting slaughter, and of its intelligence against a colossal blunder. Professors and publicists undermined the whole shaky justification for American involvement, punctured the false analogies, ridiculed the clichés and contradictions, exposed the lies. The peace movement was being swept along in a vast disaffection with the country's political leadership.

Many young radicals—hippies convinced that American society was doomed, veterans of SNCC and CORE and the S.D.S., draft resisters and mobilizers of protest demonstrations—had by this time gone far beyond mere opposition to the war in Vietnam. They were already committed to a violent revolutionary overthrow of the whole System, of which they saw Vietnam as only a symptom. But they were still a small if vocal minority.

Behind them was a great moving mass, a new generation coming out of school and college, hating the war and the draft but willing to believe what their elders had been telling them, that there were better ways than violence to effect change.

After the Chicago Democratic Convention in 1968 and the battles in the streets that punctuated it, many of these young rebels, too, would be ready to join the revolution. But first they had to try the traditional methods of reform politics. They were not convinced that peace in Vietnam and peaceful change at home could not be achieved through established democratic institutions.

Part Two

Liberalism
Limited

5 | The Senator and the Mayor

If the prime instigators of the confrontation at Chicago had all been indicted for conspiracy, Senator Eugene McCarthy should have been included. He had shifted the anti-war movement from far-out protest to what for a while looked like traditional insurgent politics. Yet the despair and sense of frustration among those who had worked for his nomination at the Democratic National Convention were a major factor in the violence that attended the convention, and the revolutionary mood that followed it.

Senator McCarthy was as much a follower as a promoter of the insurgent forces that rallied to him. It was a young lawyer, Allard K. Lowenstein, later a Congressman, only a few years past his days of student radicalism and of participation in the Mississippi civil rights movement, who organized the "Dump Johnson" movement in late 1967, and with the help of the Americans for Democratic Action and other groups of veteran liberals gave a semblance of political realism to McCarthy's quixotic candidacy. And it was the "Clean With Gene" student doorbell ringers who produced the surprising turn-out for him in the New Hampshire primary, and led the Senator as well as many serious political commentators to wonder for the first time whether perhaps he might not even become President.

In the American political system the Democratic party, no less than

63

the Republican party, is merely a loose federation of fifty state parties, and the process by which a President is nominated depends on differing procedures in each state, so the political novices who had hitched themselves to McCarthy's bandwagon had a lot to learn.

In some states with relatively open primary contests, the radicals-turned-liberals found out how important to the political process may be stuffing envelopes or baby sitting for voters taken to the polls. In other states they had to try to learn the intricacies of local caucuses and conventions by which delegates to the national convention were selected, and young amateurs found themselves confronting small town and big city politicans whose long experience made them old pros. Some of the newcomers discovered that these veteran political workers might be motivated less by the spoils of office and the hope of military-industrial contracts than by long-term personal and team loyalties, and even the fun of the game of politics itself. But if the style of the game sometimes seemed old-fashioned, the stakes were life or death, the draft or imprisonment, peace or escalating war.

For a while, early in 1968, a new day seemed to be dawning. Senator McCarthy had carried the New Hampshire primary. Senator Robert F. Kennedy entered the race, adding a whole new dimension of youthful energy to the demand for change. Then President Johnson announced he was not a candidate for re-election, and Hubert Humphrey, whose loyalty to Johnson's Vietnam policy could not wholly obscure his long record as a defender of civil rights and a former chairman of the liberal Americans for Democratic Action, became a third presidential contender. With the Republican party still divided, a shift to a more liberal national leadership seemed assured.

The youth rebellion had apparently changed the country's course, all in the space of a few months. Briefly one remembered the brave inaugural address of the other Kennedy: perhaps, after all, a new generation was in command.

But the younger Kennedy also was killed, Hubert Humphrey's speeches echoed President Johnson's, and Senator McCarthy's self-righteous aloofness left many of his young followers leaderless and dispirited. By the time the primaries were over and the delegates were gathering at Chicago, it was clear that the old Establishment was still firmly in control. The young had tried the road of conventional liberal political reform and found, or so it seemed to them, that it led nowhere. The mood, even of those few who had—almost to their own surprise—won seats at the convention, was one of disillusionment: under the traditional procedures, even the party calling itself Democratic could, it seemed, be manipulated by the existing power structure. The grim visage of Chicago's Mayor Daley seemed to dominate the convention. His police made their pressure felt both on the convention floor and in the streets around the Hilton.

Paradoxically, Johnson's absence from Chicago may have contributed to the youthful frustration and despair that erupted in Grant Park. He had been the perfect target. His old-fashioned Texas ruggedness, his lack of sensitivity to the truth, his ability to combine Bible Belt piety, New Deal liberalism, and successful pursuit of wealth and power seemed to typify everything the cultural revolution was against. It was he who had escalated the war in Vietnam, until half a million young Americans were out in East Asia fighting and dying. It was he who had made the official justification for the war as a defense of a small free country against communist aggression sound less and less credible. It was he who had exhorted the troops to bring the coonskins home.

When he vanished as a target, the whole political system by which America was ruled came under more critical scrutiny. Consciously or unconsciously the opponents of the war in Vietnam sensed that President Johnson had been as much the victim of events as their master. After all, it had been President Kennedy who had started escalating the war. The cold war as containment of communism had been the main theme since World War II, and Vietnam was only its logical application.

The thinking of the disaffected had been more and more influenced by the belief, previously popular only among communists, that America was a new colonial empire, that its policy was aggressively imperialistic. Partly this was because in Vietnam the United States had taken over the role of the French in trying to suppress an anti-colonial revolt.

Partly, the charge of imperialism stemmed from the policy, initiated under Truman, of extending American military and economic aid all over the world wherever there was a real or imagined danger of Soviet expansion or communist revolution: foreign aid necessarily meant an expanding American influence, even if justified as a counter to communist influence.

Now the Black Panthers and other militant blacks, sympathetic to the anti-colonial revolt of non-white peoples in Africa and Asia, had developed the theory that they too, the twenty million second-class American citizens of black ancestry, were victims of imperialism. All the seeming benevolence of Roosevelt's New Deal, Truman's Fair Deal, and Johnson's Great Society were, in the eyes of both black and white young radicals, a gigantic hoax, a cover-up for an exploitative and oppressive system of corporate capitalism. If that was true, then the nomination and election of a President and all the elaborate machinery of political democracy were likewise fraudulent.

The newly converted radicals pointed to what happened at Chicago as proof. The months of campaigning for Senator McCarthy seemed so much wasted effort, as the old political machines steam-rollered the convention, and Mayor Daley's police smashed the heads of those who dared protest.

Liberalism, said the new radicals, had failed. Mere reform of existing institutions would never eliminate poverty and racism, for the System, according to this view, was based on poverty and racism. It was useless to try to change it by working within the existing political parties and governmental structure, for they provided no real opportunity for participation by the poor and oppressed, and were, therefore, not truly democratic. From this conviction it was natural to draw the conclusion that a truly participatory democracy could be achieved only by revolution.

Yet even the most disaffected recognized the value of some aspects of the System they said must be destroyed. The Black Panther leader Bobby Seale was clamoring for his "constitutional rights" when he was dragged out of the courtroom at the Chicago conspiracy trial in 1969. The whole black revolt had begun with the campaign for civil rights

—equality of treatment as guaranteed by the Constitution. The major campaign against white supremacy in the mid-1960's had as its goal the power of the ballot.

The problem the young rebels, both white and black, were beginning to wrestle with after Chicago was to determine the limits of liberalism. Was the entire system of constitutional and representative democracy to be thrown out as fraudulent, or was some of it, perhaps most of it, capable of being improved, added to, expanded, to provide more benefits and wider opportunities for participation?

Democracy, presumably, begins with the ballot. But it obviously does not end there. The drowning man craves air and, for the moment, wants nothing else. If he is rescued, it will not be long before he takes air for granted. There is more to life than air. The right to vote is analogous. It is intensely precious to those who are deprived of it.

In the eighteenth century the American colonists elected their own colonial legislatures, but they were incensed that they had no representation in the English Parliament. "No taxation without representation" was the battle cry of those who dumped newly taxed tea in Boston Harbor. One hundred and fifty years later similar techniques of demonstration and disruption were practiced by suffragettes demanding votes for women. More recently, in the Deep South, blacks have given their lives in the struggle to obtain the right to register and vote. And today in southern Africa—Rhodesia, the Portuguese territories, South Africa—men and women are fighting and dying to achieve the franchise.

Actually, the ballot has been sought and cherished less as a means of participation in government than as a defense against arbitrary exercise of power by those in high position.

The ancient Athenians understood this. So did the citizens of Rome under the Republic. In our immediate tradition, the idea that absolute power must be limited goes back to the uprising of the English nobles against King John: the Magna Carta was our first Bill of Rights. Its emphasis on the restraint of power is as valid today as it was in 1215; it is as important to the ghetto radical as it was to the barons at Runnymede. Lord Acton's phrase that "power corrupts and absolute power corrupts absolutely" applies whether the power is held by a hereditary monarch or a twentieth-century dictator or simply an official of an elected government. Arrogance, indifference, greed and cruelty affect king, commissar, and petty bureaucrat alike.

Many of today's political institutions evolved not as instruments for the wielding of power, but as mechanisms for the restraint of power. This is even true of the representative assembly. A major function of the American Congress is as a check on the arbitrary power of the Executive. It has control of the purse strings, exercised in the first instance by the House of Representatives. The Senate must approve presidential appointments and ratify treaties. Congressional hearings and investigations are a way of checking on the Executive's policies and programs. Indeed, the power of the Congress to act in a positive way is far less than its power to restrain. (Sometimes, of course, it fails to do either. In 1964, for example, the Congress, with only two Senators dissenting, approved the Tonkin Gulf resolution, giving the President virtually unlimited authority to involve U.S. forces in the Vietnam war.)

Another basic democratic institution whose chief importance is also to provide a check on arbitrary power is the separation of the functions of the prosecutor and the judge. In the spectacular conspiracy trial of the Chicago Seven it was hard to tell who did more damage to that concept, the defendants who assumed the judge was biased, or the judge who persisted in proving them right. In demanding their constitutional rights while insulting the judge, the Seven seemed unaware that rights do not exist in a vacuum. Unfortunately even the pretense of judicial independence is an early casualty of any revolution, and the inalienable rights guaranteed by constitutions become empty words.

Yet the basic human right to life, liberty and the pursuit of happiness is accepted in principle everywhere in the world as an essential aspect of democracy. Similarly, freedom of conscience, speech, and assembly, and the right to criticize whatever government may be and to protest its actions, while not assuring democracy, are essential to it, as protection against the exercise of arbitrary power. These are the basic civil liberties. They are never permanently secure, and eternal vigilance is their price.

Compared to the evolution of these restraints on power—representative assemblies, an independent judiciary, and the belief that human beings are entitled to certain inalienable rights or freedoms—the idea of majority rule on the basis of "one man, one vote" is a relatively recent development. Property qualifications for the franchise were severe in the early days of our republic and disappeared only gradually, as they did in England. Maleness ceased to be a qualification only half a century ago.

The requirement that a voter must be able to read has been a stubborn survivor. Its elimination has been recently hastened by its abuse in the Southern states to prevent blacks from voting. The advent of radio and television has also made the written word less essential. An example has been set by new democratic nations such as India, where a largely illiterate population has flocked to the polls in percentages higher than in more highly developed countries. Only since World War II has America made a real effort to extend the franchise to all, regardless of skin color or language. The Voting Rights Act of 1965, which finally challenged discrimination at the state and local level directly, was a landmark in this respect.

The widening of participation in the voting process is still going on. Registration drives among the rural poor and in the ghettos continue and must continue. Nationwide enfranchisement of eighteen-year-olds is only a matter of time.

For many Americans, especially those who fled to this country from dictatorships elsewhere, voting is almost a religious sacrament. They are not seriously troubled by the fact that their options may be severely limited or that their votes are not likely to have a significant effect, and they do not seek a higher degree of participation in the process of government.

Yet many other Americans do not bother to vote, some because they are preoccupied with their own lives and have no real concern for the society in which they live, but many others because they are not convinced that voting for candidate X or candidate Y will make any difference.

The truth is that voting in itself seldom means significant participation in government.

At the bottom end of the scale, one can put voting in a dictatorship where the voter is offered a single slate of candidates but is afraid not to vote at all. Not much more significant is voting where there is a choice of candidates if every candidate is selected by a small group in the traditional "smoke-filled room."

For the more knowledgeable voter, there is perhaps a greater sense of meaningful participation in a primary election to help determine who the nominee of his party is going to be, especially if the primary offers a variety of candidates.

The electoral process comes nearer real participation in government when it concerns issues rather than representatives. Such voting is common in the approval or disapproval of state and local bond issues, and can still be seen in its pure form in New England villages small enough for direct democracy to function in the traditional "town meeting."

Early in this century, dissatisfaction with their legislatures led a number of states to adopt systems of initiative (whereby a change in the law could be put on the ballot by petition) and referendum (whereby the voters would accept or reject a proposed change in the law.) These reforms did not live up to expectations, however. The initiative was rarely used, and the referendum was shown up as having serious limitations and drawbacks. Most referendums confront the voter with the necessity of casting a yes or no vote on a complex piece of legislation which he probably understands only dimly. The result is that relatively few voters bother to register their opinions. In New York State, for instance, where sometimes ten or more different propositions and constitutional amendments are submitted to the voters in the November election, the results are determined by a small fraction of the eligible voters. There is usually a spate of editorials and letters to the editor complaining that the electorate should not be burdened with such choices, at least not with so many of them.

All this seems to point to the conclusion that, in a large and complex society, legislation by direct vote of the people is not an effective means of participation in the governing process. No substitute has been found for the representative legislature as an instrument of government. The extent to which it offers opportunity for citizen participation will depend on a number of factors, chief of which are the kind of party politics behind it and how it responds to the pressures of special interest groups.

The writers of the American Constitution hoped to escape party politics, but a two-party system quickly developed and, for all its faults, that system seems to provide a better check on arbitrary power than a one-party system, and more stability than a multiparty system.

During the 1950's and 1960's, increasing numbers of young men and women found excitement and satisfaction in becoming active in party politics. In his two presidential campaigns Adlai Stevenson inspired many to take an active part in politics for the first time. After his defeats they carried on, some to run for office themselves, some to form new kinds of issue-oriented political organizations such as the clubs of the Democratic Reform movement in New York City.

Again in 1960, 1964, and 1968, thousands of young people were roused to political activity by John and Robert Kennedy and Eugene McCarthy. The shattering and disillusioning events at Chicago in 1968 obscured the fact that some not insignificant successes had been achieved by the political activism of the Kennedy and McCarthy followers. Whether or not they drove him out, President Johnson withdrew as a candidate for re-election. They did not end the war, but they ended talk of military victory. And they set in motion major changes in the way presidential nominations would be made in the future. The unit rule whereby delegation minorities could be disfranchised was not only abolished for convention delegations themselves but, as a result of a rank-and-file revolt on the convention floor, the unit rule was abolished for all local or state meetings involved in the process of delegate selection. A commission was set up under the chairmanship of Senator George McGovern which proceeded to reexamine in depth the whole process of delegate selection and to recommend drastic changes designed to make the procedure more democratic.

What is happening within the Democratic party as a result of the 1968 Chicago convention is to a degree happening to the American political system as a whole. The Republican party may be forced to follow suit or lose young voters who might enroll under its banner. The rigidities of the past are in process of cracking and loosening up like lake ice in the spring.

The big parties remain as channels for activity, but the power of the old-fashioned "regular" party organizations is diminishing. In most areas the day of the party boss, who could dictate appointments to the highest as well as the lowliest jobs, who could reward the party faithful with nominations for seats in legislative bodies or on the bench, who could destroy any would-be rebel or even critic—that day is either gone or going.

There are a number of reasons for the decline of the political machine. One is the increasing sophistication of most voters, who are less and less inclined to vote the straight party ticket and are less tolerant of venality and corruption in public office. The prevalence of primary elections as a method of nominating candidates is another factor. Also, the emergence of social welfare programs has made the poor relatively independent of the favors of the local precinct captain. The whole process of politics and government has been brought under the spotlight of on-the-spot news coverage, especially by television. The very complexity and difficulty of most important government jobs have made it almost impossible for the old-style party hack to be appointed.

One result of all this has been an evident improvement in the quality of candidates for most offices. In recent years, for example, a remarkable number of outstanding young men and women from both parties have been elected to the Senate and the House. As their numbers swell, they are certain to demand and secure basic reforms in the stultifying and outdated rules and customs of the Congress, especially the seniority system.

Apart from the process of nominations and elections, there also has been in the last few decades a very considerable opening up of the processes of government to public scrutiny. In addition, legislators today maintain two-way communication with their constituents. More and more congressmen keep their constituents informed of what they are doing through newsletters, and solicit their opinions through district-wide questionnaires.

Obviously the fact that an elected representative is accessible—open to communication and consequent influence—makes him particularly subject to the pressures of the rich and powerful, who have always known how to cater to the vanity or taste for luxury on the part of some legislators. The vastly increased expense of campaigns makes many elected officials dependent on large contributions, made in expectation of favors to be rendered. The legislator may or may not vote as his contributor urges, but at the very least he will listen. Some members of Congress earn the reputation of being "in the pocket" of a particular lobby.

On the other hand, increasing numbers of ordinary voters now attempt to influence legislation. The most powerful lobbies, permanently stationed in Washington, are the business associations and labor unions. But to an increasing degree delegations of interested citizens and representatives of local organizations descend upon Washington and demand to see their elected representatives.

One of the few dramatic events in the 1969 session of Congress occurred when, from all over the country, school administrators and teacher and P.T.A. representatives came to insist on more federal aid for education, over and above the Administration's request, and won at least a partial victory. In 1970 their pressures overrode two vetoes.

The same increase of contact and communication between the governed and those who govern has taken place at the state and local level. While a state governor (like the President) can remain largely insulated from the public if he wishes, a mayor cannot, and certainly state and local legislators cannot. During a state legislative session, delegations travel to the state capitol daily and at least make their voices heard. They are not necessarily only spokesmen for the rich. In recent years they have included many of the poor: the National Welfare Rights Organization has, for example, become an informed and sophisticated lobby, using both conventional and unconventional tactics.

Increasingly when a neighborhood or community is to be affected by an action of government, its residents are given the chance to express their views at a public hearing. Strenuous and united community opposition to a project—the location of a highway through an urban area, for example—is not lightly disregarded by elected authorities.

With these and related developments, one might paint a rosy picture of the state of American democracy today. The processes by which the voters choose their elected officials have never been more honest, more generally representative, than they are now. Never before has government at all levels been open to such intensive scrutiny, or subject to pressure from so many different kinds of groups, from the bottom of the social scale to the top. The protection of individual rights has never been the subject of more legislative and judicial concern. In no country are individual rights significantly more secure than they are in the United States; indeed the vast majority of the peoples of the world suffer from various forms of tyranny and arbitrary power to which the Americans' political democracy stands in shining contrast. Our political institutions are clearly not a sham; they have undergone spasmodic improvement and adaptation to new circumstances, and they are clearly capable of further reform, better adaptation, wider participation by those affected.

Why then does this democracy arouse so little enthusiasm? Why has criticism reached the point of despair for many and calls for revolution from some?

In part, the sensed inadequacy of our political democracy is built in. Its institutions and techniques were never intended to enable the people to govern themselves directly. Government was a necessary evil to be kept in control by limiting the power and the functions of those to whom it was guardedly and temporarily entrusted. The government has always been "they." For our Founding Fathers "they" were the rich and well-born, believed best able to promote the common welfare because only they were competent to know what it was. Jacksonian democracy transferred government to politicians and bureaucrats, and "they" have operated the machinery of government ever since. "We, the people," participate in the process only on election day. For most of us that participation has never been much more than what was once described, before the day of voting machines, as a "stab with a pencil in the dark."

In spite of the great and increasing numbers of people who do seek to influence the processes of government, those processes are still remote, mysterious, and impersonal to the great majority. Government seems incapable of solving the most important problems: inflation, crime, hunger, pollution, war. The Congress in particular, never popular, seems unresponsive to crying needs, an institution that appears to consider itself immune from the demands for adaptation and change that have affected so many other areas of life.

Since majority rule is basic to our system, dissatisfaction has become acute for those minorities who feel that their aspirations will be perpetually blocked by the majority. Bitterness among the blacks has intensified as the very gains they have made reveal the extent to which the cards are stacked against them.

Coinciding with their rebellion is that of the young, in revolt against being drafted into what they feel is an immoral war, and, for the more thoughtful, against the policies of the cold war and the arms race which they feel are not only immoral but suicidal. They cannot belive that such policies truly represent the will of the people. If the war in Vietnam and the arms race truly represent the will of the "great silent majority," then they will refuse to accept majority rule as a definition of democracy. Many of the young rebels, with their outlandish costumes and appearance, are declaring their independence of the entire generation of their elders, majority or no. A larger number, willing to accept the outward conventions of their elders, nevertheless believe that the will of the majority has been so corrupted and manipulated as to have lost its legitimacy.

The broad picture of American life today is distorted by vivid

images of brutality, repression, and chauvinism: prosecutions of dissenters that seem clearly political in nature; a national campaign by
police officials seemingly aimed at destroying the most militant black
leadership; young men who object to the Vietnam war on moral
grounds being sent to jail or forced to flee; the Congress unable or
unwilling to control President Nixon's expansion of the war now
ravaging all of Indochina; elected officials castigating college authorities for not cracking down hard enough on student dissent and disruption; an alliance of professional military men, Pentagon suppliers, and
complaisant or jingoistic members of Congress diverting the nation's
resources from essential home needs to dangerous military superflui-
ties; profit seekers despoiling the countryside in the name of progress
to the point where the very survival of life on the planet is threatened.

These images become overwhelming. In the face of them, assur-
ances that things are better than they were, or better here than elsewhere, merely rouse the young to fury.

It is, then, not surprising that protest is turning against the whole
social order. In disillusion with the institutions and techniques of what
they have been told was democracy, many are ready to accept a major
premise of the Old Left, that democracy is impossible under capitalism. Even when they have not accepted the communist charge that
our form of democracy is merely a front for rule by the capitalist class,
they still feel that a power structure of the rich is actually running the
country for its own benefit, and that true democracy can be achieved
only under a new system. An increasing number now declare their
belief in socialism.

6 | A Meal Ticket Is Not All

Critics of the young rebels of these years have often complained that the rebels don't know what they want, but the rebels clearly know what they are against. The evils of their time are only too clear: war, racism, poverty, environmental pollution. In their desperate search for a comprehensible pattern to explain these intractable problems, they readily blame the capitalist system and look to socialism for remedy. But socialism can mean much or little. It may not be as radical a shift as it sounds.

Of the goals of the French Revolution, liberty, equality, and fraternity, Americans have always been most concerned with liberty. Equality could take care of itself, at least for those of white skin who could find new land to settle, and fraternity came naturally on the frontier. But in Europe, with its heritage of feudal classes, equality sometimes seemed more important than liberty, and fraternity was left for the millennium. Democracy was thought of less in terms of government *by* the people than as government *for* the people.

In nineteenth-century Europe the drive for democracy was carried forward by people who were more concerned with economic justice than with political liberties. They came early to the belief that democracy required fundamental changes in the economic system. Aided by an expanding franchise and the intellectual leadership of Marx and other disaffected members of the middle and upper classes, the working class sought power, through social democratic parties and labor parties pledged to socialism, however they might define it. In eastern Europe, social democracy was transformed into revolutionary communism. In the Scandinavian countries and western Europe, social democratic parties and those who adopted their platforms achieved, if not socialism, at least the common patterns of the welfare state.

The idea of social democracy, with its emphasis on equality, was certainly not absent in the early days of the American republic. The Declaration of Independence said that "all men are created equal" and Jefferson, though a slaveowner, could still rest his hopes for democracy on a society of small farmers and artisans. The absence of sharp class distinctions, in contrast to the rigidities of the Old World, was always part of the American dream. Even a wealthy or powerful man might be described as democratic if he behaved as if other people were his equals.

Yet, until the Great Depression of the 1930's, the trend in America was away from the egalitarian ideals of social democracy. Liberty was enshrined in the free enterprise system. Business became more important and powerful than government. Any regulation of business, even with respect to such obvious abuses as child labor, was denounced as socialism by the conventional wisdom, and was struck down by the courts as unconstitutional.

It is hard in 1970 to remember that in 1930, just forty years ago, a factory worker might be earning as little as five dollars a week, and he could be fired for joining a labor union. A man who lost his job had no unemployment insurance, and if he had no savings he was immediately in deep trouble. There was no social security for the aged and no insurance to take care of hospital and doctor bills.

America didn't begin to take a really serious look at herself until the winter of 1933 when the banks closed and the economy was virtually at a standstill. That year the gross national product of the country dropped to $55 billion, or a per capita disposable income of $362. (Adjusted to 1970 price levels, these figures would be $164 billion and $1,075).

Many Americans, especially the young, were profoundly shaken by these events. It seemed cruel and stupid that so many factories were standing idle and so many thousands of farms abandoned while millions of people were desperate for want of food, clothing, and shelter.

Franklin D. Roosevelt was a pragmatist, not a socialist, but his New Deal in a few years duplicated the main features of social democracy long familiar in Europe.

Step by step the functions of government increased. Social security was inaugurated, and a national minimum wage (starting at twenty-five cents an hour!) was established. Labor union activity was spurred by the Wagner Act. The first public housing was built. John Maynard Keynes's insistence that depressions could be ended by government action, using mainly monetary and fiscal tools, began to win support World War II showed what an economy stimulated and regulated by government action was capable of, and in the Employment Act of 1946, Congress made what President Truman called "a commitment to take any and all measures necessary for a healthy economy"—a concept which a few years before would have been branded as dangerous radicalism.

During the Eisenhower administration, the government, frightened by the first Soviet satellite, embarked on a major program of federal aid for education in the sciences, mathematics, and foreign languages. Under John F. Kennedy, federal programs to assist economically depressed areas were launched, and vocational training became a recognized federal government function. President Johnson declared war on poverty and persuaded Congress to set up a special agency for the purpose, operating with the "maximum feasible participation" of the poor. After years of effective propaganda against "socialized medicine" by the American Medical Association, Medicare for the aging and Medicaid for the poor were enacted. Massive federal aid for elementary and secondary education followed. By 1968 the Democratic party and some liberal Republicans were calling for the Federal government to be the employer of last resort. By 1969 a national consensus was emerging that hunger in America was intolerable, and that a minimum income for all must be guaranteed.

The welfare state, long denounced, had arrived.

For the Negro population of the country, the New Deal had little to offer beyond the assertion that the government should take positive action to assure civil rights for minorities. As early as 1941 President Roosevelt established a Fair Employment Practices Committee, though it had little power. But in the postwar period the Supreme Court, for so long a bastion of conservatism, became a major force for change as it overruled its own "separate but equal" doctrine and demanded an end to segregation in public facilities and schools. The once-impregnable barrier of the Senate filibuster was finally cracked in 1964 when enforceable civil rights laws were enacted. At long last equality of rights—economic and social rights having to do with jobs, housing, education, transportation, and public accommodations, as well as political rights—seemed within reach.

For the middle-aged liberal, battle-scarred from years of struggle, these accomplishments represent progress that no one could have predicted back in 1933. Yet even to him our social and economic problems often seem worse today than they were then, in spite of affluence.

The decade of the seventies opened with a general sense of apprehension rather than confidence. In part this sense of overwhelming social problems stems from a greater awareness. Television, for good or ill, has helped to prod the national conscience. The protests of the young, both black and white, who know nothing of past battles and earlier social ills surmounted, have sensitized their elders to present injustice and deprivation.

But in part the deterioration is real: tensions and dangers have increased, not diminished.

It is as if, with an accelerating rate of social change, new social problems rise faster than the old can be solved.

The problem of massive unemployment that wreaked havoc in the 1930's has been solved in all advanced countries, but as strategic monetary and fiscal controls achieve full employment, inflationary pressures become critical. In the cities, despite social security, welfare aid, public housing, and a vast expansion of public health and public education, the overwhelming impression is of physical and social decay. The spread of drugs, which to some of the young has appeared as liberation, has had an explosive effect on violent crime. As preventable disease declines and incomes mount, the environment becomes choked with people and their wastes.

Yet this proliferation of problems is not new. Every advance in the physical sciences has raised more questions than it has solved, and there is no reason to despair if advances in the social sciences do the same. They only open up new challenges for new generations.

Not one of the social problems of our time is beyond our capacity to solve.

Many of the evils that beset us can be eradicated if we can reach a major goal of the welfare state toward which we have been moving: the elimination of poverty. We have the technology and the resources to do it. There is no reason why we cannot provide to all Americans, including the weak and helpless and those with few talents or none at all, a fair share of this world's goods. There is no reason why every child who wants it cannot be given the opportunity of a college education. There is no reason why every family in this country should not have a decent place to live. There is no reason why adequate medical care should not be universal.

The war on poverty is far from won, but it has not been abandoned, and until it is won no society can any longer consider itself truly democratic. Certainly the complete abolition of hunger and physical want is within immediate reach. Controls over the distribution of the national product through taxation, subsidies, and the regulation of private enterprise have helped to produce a vast majority of reasonably well-to-do, middle-class citizens. Equality of income is hardly a sensible goal, for human needs are not equal, and the economic incentive which rewards effort and enhances productivity is so deeply rooted in human nature that differentials of pay will exist in any economic or social order we can foresee. But a floor under income is now close to acceptance as a national policy, and equality of economic opportunity is acknowledged to be as fundamental a right as legal and political equality.

When a family becomes truly affluent, the level of economic well-being of each of its members does not depend on fortuitous circumstances of age or capacity or productivity; so when a society becomes truly affluent each of its members could be assured affluence without regard to his contribution.

How nearly we may in time approach such a utopian-sounding goal need not now concern us. What is important is to recognize that it is a reasonable and necessary goal for this country, and that it is not at all beyond human capacity as an achievable worldwide goal. Despite the dangers that beset us, we are moving in that direction. We should further recognize that, call it the welfare state or social democracy or socialism or what you will, the assurance of material well-being to all is a logical extension of the democratic idea that all men are members of the commonwealth.

Yet if democracy were no more than universal affluence it would be as unsatisfying a social goal as democracy limited to the ballot box.

The campus radicals who have turned in anger against their well-to-do parents may grossly underrate the significance of what older generations have achieved, in broadening and extending economic opportunity and making material well-being more nearly universal. But they are thoroughly justified in their feeling that this is far from providing a good life, either for them or their contemporaries. Man does not live by bread alone. The welfare state, even if all its goals are achieved, is not necessarily a great society.

Rugged individualism is an antiquated principle in economic affairs, but it is a valid aspect of the good life. Paternalism, however benevolent, is an indignity. When it becomes the impersonal paternalism of the state the indignity is compounded. The youthful rebel against paternalism, in the home or on the campus, can sympathize with the welfare recipient who feels no more grateful to the bureaucrat of a public welfare department than to the "do-gooder" of private charity.

The almsgiver was at least a recognizable individual. The welfare state is an impersonal bureaucratic machine, inexorably proliferating under the impact of "Parkinson's Law," tangling us all in red tape, burying us under mountains of paper. The panic that can grip even the most highly educated of us when confronted with the filling out of a new form for registering a motor vehicle, or paying a tax, or tracing a lost social security check, is a measure of the tyranny of administrative bureaucracy.

In the Soviet Union and the so-called People's Democracies, where the institutions and techniques of political democracy have been ignored because they were thought designed only for capitalist profit, the tyranny of the bureaucrat is likely to be unrelieved. No matter how benevolent communist bureaucrats may be or become, in providing what they believe is good for their charges, the atmosphere will still be stifling.

The Soviet Establishment in its moral and cultural strictures may reflect the will of the majority more nearly than does the American Establishment, if only because it has a greater power to shape that majority will. So shaped, the demos can be as great a tyrant as an individual dictator.

In America we remain dedicated to the egalitarian democracy admired by De Tocqueville early in our history. But De Tocqueville also feared the dead hand of the majority. We need not give up the values or the benefits of social democracy, but we have to recognize its limitations. Even if the welfare state were wholly successful in meeting all the material wants of all its members, it would be little more satisfying than a society dominated, as some think ours is today, by corporate bureaucracies seeking only private profit.

The young radicals of today seem ready to discard all that has been gained and can still be gained in the way of economic equality and social democracy, just as they show a reckless lack of regard for the liberties and opportunities of political democracy. But they recognize that life is hardly worth living, and society has no meaning, if their share is limited to a ballot and a meal ticket.

Part | Three

Radical
Response

7 | The Movement

The turbulence of the 1960's was not merely in protest against the ancient evils of racism and war. It was also in protest against the slowness of reform. The young were in revolt against their liberal elders and had turned against the liberal movement because liberalism seemed too slow.

A liberal Supreme Court had decreed the end of discrimination "with all deliberate speed," but the new militants of the civil rights movement wanted "Freedom Now." Liberal professors had been trying to persuade the President to de-escalate Vietnam, but their students wanted the war ended now. Liberal politicians had advanced programs to aid the disadvantaged, reforms that would mitigate urban blight, but young radicals were demanding a whole new social order.

Since those in power would not or could not move, the rebels began thinking of power for themselves—black power, student power. But how could blacks alone, or students alone, change society? What if they joined forces? Might others join them? The cultural and moral rebels against traditional standards might provide recruits. Wavering liberals might be drawn in, as they were radicalized by confrontations on campus and in the streets.

More and more of the young in the different centers of unrest began talking about "the movement." For some it was merely an expression

87

of a common faith in fundamental social change. For those who believed that nothing short of revolution could cure the ills of society, the movement was the organization that must be prepared to take advantage of a revolutionary situation when it arose.

By the end of the turbulent 1960's there had been efforts to organize what was being called the New Left. The Old Left, the splintered remnants of the Russian inspired Communist movement, had little appeal for the new radicals. Even the more authentic radical tradition, springing from the Jeffersonian doctrine of the right of people to change their form of government by revolution, seemed to have only slight appeal to a generation that was largely focused on the present and the future, not the past.

Yet there was precedent for the effort to bring together the forces of discontent, if not for purposes of revolution, at least in a new political party. Since the Civil War a number of independent political movements had briefly challenged the established political parties. The Grangers, the Greenbackers, the People's party, the Progressives, were mostly sparked by frontier farmers rebelling against the power of eastern money. Labor unrest added a new note. By 1900 the ideas of Marxist socialism, brought to eastern cities mainly by recent immigrants, had combined with the more utopian dreams of the western Populists in the vision of a "cooperative commonwealth" which would replace the capitalist system.

The great depression of the 1930's, when capitalism seemed in final collapse, spawned a variety of insurgent movements and third parties. There was a Farmer-Labor party and a Commonwealth Federation and a Utopian Society. A Communist party, inspired and no doubt financially assisted by the Bolsheviks after their seizure of power in Russia, made some converts among American workers, and even more among left-wing writers and intellectuals. There were the brief flare-ups of Huey Long's Share the Wealth movement, the Silver Shirts, and Father Coughlin's Union party, all expressing the kind of middle-class fear of bankers and communists alike that had put Mussolini and Hitler in power in Europe.

Yet, for all their turbulence, American political institutions had remarkable stability. Third-party movements came and went, but the Republican and Democratic parties continued to dominate the political scene. Despite hysteria over the communist menace at home and abroad, the American Communist party remained insignificant. Revolutions might sweep the rest of the world, empires might fall and economic systems be transformed, but American political institutions seemed eternal.

In the 1960's, however, as dissenting voices became more numerous and revolt against established ways and established insitutions became widespread, there was again talk of a new politics.

As early as 1964, leaders of the Mississippi campaign to register Negro voters had challenged the state's lily-white delegation to the National Democratic Convention at Atlantic City, and sought recognition as the Freedom Democratic party.

Efforts to unite the anti-war forces in a new political party for the off-year elections were made in 1966, and a number of independent candidates ran for the House of Representatives and the Senate in Massachusetts, New Jersey, and elsewhere. None of them achieved sufficient results to continue more than a marginal existence as names on a letterhead. Their central theme was peace in Vietnam, and though they sought support in the ghettos, militant blacks showed little interest.

The first nation-wide effort to bring together all of the new dissident elements in a common political front was the National Conference for New Politics, which held a convention in Chicago at the end of the violent summer of 1967. It was a chaotic gathering of newly militant blacks and young white radicals from the peace movement and campus revolts. To the blacks their own drive for black power was central; all other issues, even the Vietnam war, were peripheral. Though representatives of various student and radical peace movements were far more numerous than the blacks, the latter formed a "black caucus," insisted on equal representation of whites and blacks, and demanded that their statement of aims, which included condemnation of "Zionist imperialism," be accepted or they would leave the gathering. The whites surrendered, putting unity of "the movement" above all else. But it was a futile gesture. The militant blacks had only emphasized how difficult it was to achieve unity. There was no real agreement on common political action or even common aims, and nothing came of the convention.

Within the student movements and the peace movements, the battle went on between those who considered themselves radicals, because they believed in basic changes in the whole social and economic system, and those who still accepted the liberal methods of gradual and piecemeal reform. Cutting across that conflict was the division between the inheritors of the socialist tradition, who believed the working class must take power if the necessary changes were to be made, and those, like the Weatherman and Revolutionary Youth movements of S.D.S., who felt the Marxist-Leninist theories were out of date and ill-adapted to American conditions. And, finally, the militants who accepted violence as unavoidable in the making of fundamental change confronted those who were convinced that non-violence must be both means and end.

During the following months, culminating in the Democratic convention in Chicago, the more moderate elements channeled their energies behind Senator McCarthy and Senator Kennedy. The more radical were involved in increasingly bitter demonstrations against the war, confrontations on campuses, and ghetto battles.

The nearest approach to a united political party of the New Left was the Peace and Freedom party, based in California but appearing on the ballot in 1968 in some other areas. Its inspiration came from the Black Panthers. The Black Panther party had first appeared two years before in Lowndes County, Alabama, and in Oakland, California, organized by militant blacks who were convinced that any attempt to achieve black power without being prepared to meet violence would end in genocide. The Oakland group under Bobby Seale and Huey Newton had differed from other black militants in that they were willing to ally themselves with white radicals. Now in the summer of 1968 a combination of militant anti-war groups, campus radicals, and Panthers secured the 100,000 signatures needed in California to put the name of Eldridge Cleaver, author and Black Panther leader, then trying to stave off imprisonment for parole violation, on the ballot as a candidate for President. Jerry Rubin, later one of the "Chicago Seven," was the candidate for Vice-President. But the party's impact on the campaign was negligible. In contrast, the "white backlash" party of Governor George C. Wallace of Alabama was on the ballot in virtually every state, and actually carried five states on Election Day.

By the end of 1968 the New Left, despite all the revolutionary talk, was little more than an idea. It might still call itself the Movement but it was a movement without organization. Only the loosest sort of alliance remained between the radical Students for a Democratic Society, the radicals of the peace movement, typified by the Resistance, and the militant blacks, represented by the Black Panthers. But while the more thoughtful of the young radicals began to reassess the practicality of their ideas of revolution, the hyperactive began tearing their own organizations apart. In any radical movement factional splintering seems to be a natural reaction to failure.

The S.D.S. offered the clearest example of the problems of the New Left. When it was founded in 1962, the drama of the civil rights movement and mounting opposition to the war in Vietnam had begun to stir the young to a new militancy. Losing faith in New Deal liberalism, they were increasingly attracted by some of the Marxist ideas of a working class revolt against capitalism which had marked the previous period of campus radicalism, back in the 1930's.

To the new student movement, suppression of any popular revolt against colonialism or economic imperialism was implicit in America's cold war policy. The S.D.S. was, therefore, tolerant of communist "wars of liberation." Yet it was too much aware of the end products of the Russian Revolution to be attracted to the old communist movement. Kremlin militarists had been matching America's bombs with superbombs of their own. Communist bureaucrats enforced a rigid orthodoxy in morals and the arts, and controlled all aspects of life to a degree the new radicals found as stifling as what they were rebelling against in America. Then, in the very same month that Mayor Daley's police were cracking the heads of dissenters at

Chicago, the Soviet Army undertook to smash dissent in its Czech satellite, and the concept of a "People's Democracy" took on a quality of hypocrisy to which the American radical ear was already critically attuned.

Yet non-Russian communism retained its appeal. Castro and Che Guevara, the bearded romantics of communist Cuba, had a particular attraction for young American radicals, also bearded, also romantic. So did Mao Tse-tung, if only because his aura of mystery and the cryptic magic of his published *Thoughts* so contrasted with the prosaic dullness of the Soviet leadership. Then, too, his emphasis on communes as a counterweight to bureaucrats appealed to those who were seeking escape from corporate bigness. Even more attractive as a communist leader, Ho Chi-minh became almost a father figure to some of the leftists.

Still there was little these new heroes of the communist left could offer American radicalism by way of program. While their glorification of guerrilla warfare held a growing fascination for many impatient radicals, the conditions of their struggles for power were remote from those confronting American student rebels. Leninist doctrines, moreover, called for a kind of disciplined thinking that had little appeal.

The anti-intellectualism that pervaded much of the cultural revolt, particularly in its hippie aspects, was unfavorable to disciplined thinking. Invective tended to be taken by much of the New Left as a substitute for critical analysis. Some of the radical student leaders like Carl Oglesby in the early period of the S.D.S. had produced significant critical writing, but most of the young radicals seemed to have more confidence in their emotional reactions than in what they considered sterile intellectualizing. Then, too, having condemned an older generation whose pronouncements had lost credibility, and having declared their mistrust of anyone over thirty, many were inclined to believe that their own generation was the first to discover the imperfections of the social order. One of the few older critics who did have an influence, Herbert Marcuse, tended to reinforce their conviction that the revolution would define its methods and its goals as it went along: "The program for the revolution is the revolution," he said.

Moreover, student radicals were never sure who their enemy was. Young blacks fighting for recognition could identify a "white power structure," particularly in Southern cities, but their white supporters on northern campuses could only echo the phrase, without being sure who or what it was. War resisters similarly picked up Eisenhower's warning against the "military-industrial complex" and identified its more obvious components, but when organized labor turned out to be one of the components, it was not easy to see where one's attack should begin.

As university administrations became a target and called in the police for protection, the student left began to develop a belief in a vast and malevolent conspiracy: the power to wage war, to maintain a profitable arms race, and to threaten rebellious students and ghetto rebels with enslavement, even genocide, was thought of as concentrated in the hands of a few shadowy figures meeting in secret.

The evils against which the student radicals fulminated were real. But the Establishment which they aimed to overthrow was in some ways little more than a creation of their imaginations. Separate elements of the Establishment, again, were real enough—the Pentagon, the great corporations, the opinion moulders—but how they fitted together, how decisions were made, and what could be done to produce better decisions seemed beyond explanation. Or explanations differed so widely that they could not be reconciled.

With so little accepted social theory available to unify it, the movement, of which the S.D.S. was the most vivid expression, began to splinter into fragments.

At the S.D.S. convention in the summer of 1969, the most orthodox Marxist element, the Trotskyist Progressive Labor movement, insisting most strictly that the industrial working class must make the revolution, first broke away. Then the militant blacks of the Panther party revolted against what they felt was the unrealistic theorizing of the ultra-left white radicals, and went their own way. Finally the romantic extremists, called "Weathermen," from a line of a Bob Dylan song—"You don't need a weatherman to know which way the wind blows"—who urged guerrilla warfare and fighting in the streets as the only way to stir the masses to action, broke with another faction, the Revolutionary Youth Movement. This group also believed in "revolutionary action" but felt that overt violence was premature and would alienate more of the poor and oppressed than it won over. Each faction claimed to be the S.D.S. and denounced the other.

As had happened occasionally in the long history of European revolutionary movements, frustration and isolation and extremism seemed to feed on each other. Lenin had called the tendency "infantile leftism." Like nineteenth-century Russian anarchists, whose beards and long hair had become stock features of caricature, some of the young American amateurs of revolution were beginning to adopt bombing as a tactic. Instruction sheets for the manufacture of bombs circulated widely. Fire bombs and explosives were set off in chain stores, corporate offices and university buildings. Property, not life, was the target, but some deaths occurred, especially among the revolutionaries themselves. At the same time, an increasing number of the restless young, even if their movement was still inchoate, were beginning to talk less glibly about revolution and to dig more deeply into what it meant.

While the more politically conscious and intellectually sophisticated of the young radicals have been trying to discover how they can weld together the different elements of the movement into an effective political force, those whose only radicalism is in their attitudes and life modes may constitute no less effective a force for social change. These participants in the cultural, esthetic, and moral revolt of youth may or may not identify with the radical activists, but they are nonetheless part of the movement, in fact the largest part. And they may well have a more decisive impact in altering the patterns of organized living than those who are thinking in terms of political power.

The more visible signs of their rebellion, such as their length of hair, may be no more than passing styles. But the underlying changes in their view of the meaning of life, their evaluation of civilization, and of man's place in the universe are profound and may well be lasting.

These changes in attitude, of course, provide much of the motive force for the activists in the movement, but they are felt by a much larger segment of the younger generation, even if the latter seem to belong to the "great silent majority." Militant protests against the draft, for instance, and against the war in Vietnam represent more than merely the resistance of a vocal minority to a particular war and its impact on them: they reflect a widespread repudiation by the young of the whole concept of war as a legitimate human activity.

Similarly, the campus revolt is the spearhead of a mounting demand by all young people that they be treated as people. And the Black Panthers, however few in actual numbers, are voicing the demand of all black people that they be treated as people.

Clearly, these demands and the underlying changes in American attitudes which they signify have their counterparts throughout the world. The more advanced countries of the "free world"—western Europe, and Japan—have seen many of the same symptoms of a new generation in revolt against old ways. Styles of dress and language and sexual behavior pay little heed to national boundaries. Traditional patterns in the relations between generations and between sexes are different in different European capitals, and diverge most markedly in Japan, but the new patterns of thought and behavior that are replacing them tend to be everywhere similar. Student rebellions against authoritarian university structures and conservative control over higher education have been even more violent in Paris and in Tokyo than on any American campus.

In eastern Europe and the Soviet Union discipline is much tighter, but the students of Prague defied the Soviet colossus even in the name of its own communist creed. In the off-again–on-again liberalization of Soviet communism since the death of Stalin, pressure for more freedom has been building up in the new and vastly expanded elite of the educated young.

Even the spectacular "proletarian cultural revolution" of 1965–1968 in China, though initiated and manipulated by Mao Tse-tung at the center of power, developed a spontaneity that was similar to youthful revolts elsewhere. The attack by students on the old party bureaucracy seemed to need little prodding from Peking; in fact it got so out of hand that Chairman Mao had finally to use his checkrein and remind the young they were still in harness.

In the poorer parts of the world, among the less developed nations now emerging from traditionalism and a colonial status, educated elites, often centering in universities, share the beliefs and attitudes of young radicals in the wealthier countries. However, these student radicals in Latin America, black Africa, and Southeast Asia find their countries already seething with revolution for reasons far removed from those agitating American campuses. They can find a mass base, among disaffected rural and urban poor, and can identify landowners, moneylenders, foreign corporations, and alien armies as common enemies.

The whole world, then, seems to confirm American radicals in their belief that the revolution they have espoused is a world revolution. Yet its outlines are confused and shadowy. When Czech students in 1967 confronted Soviet tanks marked with the Communist hammer and sickle, whose was the revolution? When hundreds of Left Bank students, with the collapse of the Sorbonne insurrection in 1968, joined the weekend exodus by car and motorscooter to the country around Paris, what was the real nature of the social transformation of which they were a part?

These questions are particularly baffling to those of the new generation of radicals who are turning to the Marxist theories of the Old Left. After all, Marx promised a world revolution, and now at length it appears to be at hand. Yet is it the one he predicted?

Analyzing the economic and social consequences of new modes of industrial production a hundred years ago, Marx had forecast a time when the whole capitalist system would break down, and the many poor and oppressed of the world would rise up against their capitalist masters.

Much of the turmoil around the globe has no doubt followed economic changes resulting from the application of scientific thinking to industry and the development of new technologies. And the communist movement which Marx founded has spread over half the globe. Yet the revolution he expected, in the countries of advanced industrialization, never took place. Only the peasantry in undeveloped countries acted the revolutionary role originally prescribed for the industrial proletariat.

In America and the West, automation has steadily diminished the role of muscle power. The expansion of occupations in the distribution of the products of industry and in services has added masses of white-collar workers, and blue-collar workers in many industries have, through effective collective bargaining, tripled and quadrupled their real wages. Business, industry and government have all produced vast bureaucracies, none the smaller because of the omnipresence of the computer. These tendencies have combined to make the more advanced countries overwhelmingly middle-class.

At the same time, the instabilities of economies given to alternations of "boom and bust"—what Marx and his followers saw as "contradictions" that would end in the total collapse of the capitalist system—were gradually overcome. The laissez-faire capitalism of the early nineteenth century gave way to an increasingly mixed, half-socialist, half-capitalist managed economy, able to prevent the cataclysmic depressions of the past and to afford the social welfare programs, old age pensions, health insurance and other alleviations of poverty known as the welfare state.

That it was also a warfare state, dependent on an escalating arms race for prosperity, might be argued by those who still clung to Marxist economics and interpretation of history, and even by more contemporary critics. But this view seemed contradicted by the performance of the stock market in relation to the Vietnam war—up with news suggesting peace, down with the reverse.

In any case, there was no doubt that the profound social changes initiated by the machine and known as the industrial revolution, far from slowing down, had continued to accelerate, and that the turbulence of the 1960's was an aspect of that revolution. But what was happening in the world hardly conformed to Marx's nineteenth-century expectations.

The turbulence was more closely related to an older historical trend, the eighteenth-century democratic and egalitarian movement. When the Black Panthers lifted a whole paragraph from the Declaration of Independence, on the inherent right of people to overthrow their government, and incorporated it in their statement of purposes, they were going back to an earlier revolutionary tradition. So were some of the student radicals. Democratic ideas and impulses appear throughout history, but the present democratic trend is, at most, three centuries old in western Europe, and is only now reaching some parts of the world for the first time. It is not so much a single revolution as the source of a whole crop of revolutions.

The idea that every human being is worthy of consideration, and entitled to share in determining his own destiny, has run counter to the dehumanizing trends of the machine age. But it owes much to science and the machine. Those who have been loudest in their criticism of the advance of technology often have been those who have benefited most from the advances they criticize. As usual, it has been the privileged and the wealthy who have had the leisure to cultivate their tastes. Many of the young rebels of today, inspired by Thoreau's example of a return to nature, have driven their own cars to secluded refuges, solitary or communal, or to a rock music festival in a pasture. They are making a legitimate protest against the machine and the computer. But the machine and the computer have been not only dehumanizing; they have been immensely liberating.

Democratic revolution would have been impossible without the industrial revolution. The more advanced the technology, the more education required for its development and utilization. Campus radicals may protest the tendency of university trustees to think of the university as a factory for training robots to man the corporate structure; however, there would be few rebels and few campuses on which to rebel if modern industry had not promoted a great expansion of higher education. In the same way the creation of an advanced industrial technology in the Soviet Union may have written the death warrant of the totalitarian dictatorship by which it was achieved, as a whole generation has been given opportunities for higher education.

The egalitarian notion that no one is born to be a slave or a serf and that every human being has inalienable rights has gradually spread around the world. Traditionalist societies, in which most men accept the station into which they were born as a part of the order of nature, can still be found in the less developed parts of the world. But the old-fashioned idea that all men are created equal, which has toppled thrones and dissolved empires in the past, is still at work. And the same notion is behind much of the turmoil in the advanced nations.

While the egalitarian concept has provided the principal fuel for the great revolutions of the last two hundred years, it has also promoted the more gradual social changes of the liberal movements of the nineteenth century, which expanded the suffrage and went on to the social welfare legislation of western Europe at the turn of the century, the American New Deal a generation later, and the present welfare state.

What we have we take for granted. It is both a strength and a weakness of radical movements of today that they believe the past to have little relevance to the present. Those concerned enough to risk their comforts, if not their lives, in fighting the evils that beset the world today—war, racism, exploitation and spoliation—cannot be expected to take satisfaction in the achievements of the radical movements of the past hundred years. They are not likely to recognize that what is called liberalism at one time and place may have been and may yet be the most revolutionary kind of radicalism at another. And even if they recognize their debt to the liberal ideas and movements of the past, they are now convinced that peaceful and gradual change can no longer accomplish what needs to be done.

When Black Panthers or the S.D.S. talk of revolution they are not thinking merely symbolically. The long slow process by which human rights and opportunities have been expanded under the impact of technological change and democratic liberalism may in a long perspective be thought of as a revolution, but they are thinking of something far more dramatic.

What they obviously have in mind is a sudden change in the society as a whole. They will not accept mere piecemeal or gradual change. Their aim is a shift of power from those now holding it to those they feel they represent. To them the movement means a violent revolution.

8 | Come the Revolution

The mental image conjured up by the word "revolution," in the minds of most of the young radicals, is largely derived from the French and Russian revolutions. The picture is of armed mobs in the streets, barricades, assaults on prisons or palaces. Behind the melodrama is the overthrow of a whole social and governmental structure, and the seizure of power by organized revolutionists.

If they have a model it is likely to be the Russian Revolution, in which a small disciplined group took advantage of popular unrest and seized political power by force. Not that today's radicals have the same aims as the Bolsheviks, or that they approve of either the methods used or the results attained. But they agree with the communists that the existing power structure will not yield without a violent struggle. They are no longer asking whether the changes they desire can be made within the existing political system. They are asking how a revolution is made.

How is power taken from those who have it? Despite all the revolutionary talk and a growing feeling of insecurity among those who have influence and power in this country, no clear answer has yet emerged.

Revolutionary seizures of power in many other countries within recent memory provide material for comparative analysis. Revolution has been endemic in Latin America, with Bolivia perhaps the extreme

101

example of a country where revolutionary changes in regime have averaged more than one a year. Many of these have been mere palace revolutions, sometimes bloodless, in which rival personalities have gained temporary ascendancy within an authoritarian regime which remains substantially unchanged.

A pattern that has been repeated many times, not only in Latin America but in many of the developing countries of Africa and Asia, is the seizure of power by the armed forces, or a portion of them, at the expense of civilian politicians. Traditionally the military caste has been recruited from and allied with the landed gentry, and has supported aristocratic and propertied classes threatened by democratic movements from below. With the growth of new middle classes and the spread of education, the officer class is now more likely to be close to social discontent, and less a product of established privilege. A military regime may seek to advance the interests of the "new" technical and bureaucratic middle classes from which its members come, and it may, therefore, be more progressive than reactionary.

Where these new middle classes are themselves in a condition of extreme insecurity, and are threatened by a real or imagined communist take-over, a seizure of power by the military may result in a fascist type of regime, as with Franco's Spain in the late 1930's. But in the case of the Perón revolution in Argentina in the 1940's, labor gave the military elements substantial support. In a recent military coup in Peru, a constitutional regime, which had genuinely liberal leadership in President Belaúnde Terry but was hampered by its dependence on landowning and financial interests, gave way to a group of young officers demanding land reform, programs for the rural and city poor, and seizure of American industries. Another notable example of a military take-over combined with many features of a social revolution was that by which Nasser came to power in Egypt.

None of these, however, has much bearing on the possibilities of revolution in the United States. The only military revolt that might have such a bearing was the overthrow of France's Fourth Republic in 1950, when army officers, blaming civilian politics for France's inability to keep Algeria in subjection, turned power over to General de Gaulle, who then diverted the revolt to his own version of national glory.

A plausible parallel can be pictured in the United States with a take-over of the national government by the Pentagon. This has been the subject of vivid novels and movies, and is not wholly inconceivable. The frustrations of the war in Vietnam, particularly to a military leadership persuaded that victory would be possible if only the people and the politicians would leave them alone, might provide the counterpart to the Algerian crisis. A white middle-class backlash against pacifists, student radicals, and militant blacks would even provide the setting for a fascist scenario, complete with the "stab in the back" theme which so well served Nazi demagogy. Other ingredients of Hitler's seizure of power—fighting in the streets, the economic strains of inflation, and the growing sense of a breakdown of public order— might convince American military leaders that only they could save the country from destruction and disintegration.

But this, needless to say, is not the kind of revolution those radicals who see mounting violence as an opportunity have in mind.

If the New Left in this country is to be realistic it must consider the class character of revolution: it must be able to say what class is now in power, and what class could take power. It does not have to follow Marx and his socialist and communist successors to their nineteenth-century conclusion that only the industrial working class can overthrow the capitalist class and make a revolution. But it cannot escape what is valid in the Marxist analysis of history as a history of class struggle.

In class terms the great French Revolution marked the end of an aristocracy based on land, and the beginning of rule by a bourgeoisie based on industry and trade. The long drawn out but equally convulsive English Revolution of the previous century, and the American Revolution, which immediately preceded the French, involved various religious and political issues, yet the shift of power to new classes of merchants and businessmen is an essential aspect of those major social revolutions. Next on the stage of history, according to Marx, was to be the industrial working class.

However valid it once was, this prediction is a poor guide to contemporary social change. The industrial working class, after long and bitter struggles, won the right to organize in unions, and has since achieved such progress in the advanced Western countries, both in terms of standards of living and of political power, as to give it a vested interest in things as they are. It has long had much more to lose than its "chains," despite the Communist Manifesto.

Then, again, in emphasizing the working class as the instrument of social change, the Marxists overlooked the importance of the new middle classes of white collar workers in the service and distributive trades, the bureaucrats and technicians. In an expanding industrial civilization, these were becoming more numerous than the manual workers. A militant labor movement, with Marxist leaders committed to a socialist revolution, might frighten the new middle classes into organizing to defend their own interests. Whether one calls Fascism revolutionary or counter-revolutionary, there is no doubt that the Italian Fascists under Mussolini and Hitler's Nazis in Germany came from the middle classes, roused to action by the breakdown of the economy and the turmoil that followed World War I.

In recent years, as blue collar workers have achieved security and rising standards of living they have been absorbed into the white collar way of life, and in the advanced countries the factory worker may be as staunchly middle-class as the office worker.

Those who would organize class interests for social revolution can no longer overlook that it is the new middle classes which are now dominant. The Marxists had failed to apply their own social analysis to these new middle classes.

A second major error of the Marxists stemmed from their failure to remember that power corrupts. The self-righteous intolerance of the communist leaders who seized power in Russia during World War I, their willingness to use any means, being certain of the rightness of their ultimate ends, led directly to the use of terror, secret police, slave labor camps, and all the horrors of Stalinist totalitarianism. The Soviet Union became a "utopia in chains." And the Communist party, which was to be the temporary instrument for working class rule, acquired a vested interest in its power: the new class that came to power was not the working class but the vast bureaucracy of the Party and of economic management.

There was nothing peculiarly Russian about the Stalinist dictatorship. Its experience was later mirrored in communist China, and in the communist regimes of eastern Europe. The latter were, in varying degrees, closer to the liberal democracy of the West, and even the Soviet Union ultimately demonstrated that the excesses of revolutionary dictatorship do not last forever: a mellowing or liberalizing trend sets in, leading to repeated efforts of those in power to strike it down. But, at best, a whole generation, even two, have seen their hope of freedom deferred.

The New Left in America has no desire to repeat the communist experience. It is sophisticated enough to know that nineteenth-century conceptions of an industrial proletariat are largely irrelevant today. But if the working class is ruled out, is there any other new class or group of classes which may be able to make a revolution?

Can students be considered such a class? Students have played an important part in revolutions elsewhere, and in no other country and at no other time has the student class been as numerous as it is in America today. Never before has the university campus, which is the base of operations for the student revolt, been as important to the social order as a whole. Business management, science and technology, and the huge empire of the makers and users of weapons depend on institutionalized learning and research in our "multiversities." Some of the theorists of the New Left have ingeniously modified Marxist concepts to make of the students an exploited class whose specialized training represents a new kind of labor power from which to extract profit.

Yet even if student radicals were able, as they have sometimes boasted, to bring the universities to a "grinding halt," the very fact that they are students, and therefore are only preparing to operate the country's productive plant rather than being a part of its essential functioning, means they are out of reach of any strategic controls. As students, they can hardly become the dominant class.

A closer parallel to Marx's proletariat is an increasingly militant and organized black population, concentrated in the big industrial cities, rendered desperate by the increasing tensions and insoluble problems of the ghetto. Thus the black segment of society already has many of the attributes of a revolutionary class.

Yet only the most fanatical visionary would seriously forecast that the black population as a class could become dominant in this country. It constitutes only eleven percent of the total population, and while no one would claim that a majority is needed to make a revolution, this particular minority is as disadvantaged for purposes of establishing its political power over the rest as it is for economic success. Its lack of an economic base helps explain why some of the more despairing of the black leaders talk emotionally of a white policy of genocide.

The New Left may think of a coalition of student radicals and black militants as the vanguard of the revolution, but they know they need a broader class base. Could they find it among the more disaffected of the so-called new middle classes? Might these, under certain conditions, become the instrument of a true revolution?

Perhaps that is where the revolt of the young, considered in its wider aspects and not simply as a campus rebellion, takes on its greatest significance. The revolt of those under thirty is mainly a revolt of the sons and daughters of the new middle classes. Their elders are now overwhelmingly the dominant element in American society and the American economy, in point of number if not of power.

These members of a new bourgeoisie are far from wanting to overturn the system which has given them cars and TV sets and homes in the suburbs. But for their rebellious sons and daughters there is grave dissatisfaction with their way of life, a feeling that life has no meaning, no purpose. Whether these sons and daughters, the more advanced of whom are now using revolutionary phrases, will be able in a few years, when they move into positions of influence, to become the spearhead of a true social revolution, perhaps in alliance with the new educated elite from the ghetto—this question has yet to be answered.

The answer might be clearer if another question were first answered: who has the power now—who is at the controls? What, as a matter of fact, is the power structure, the Establishment, which the New Left wants to overthrow?

Here the answers given by the would-be revolutionists are particularly vague. The wealthy are always a legitimate target, and there is plenty of careful social analysis, as well as invective, concerned with the rich and the very rich. Radicalism has always used "malefactors of great wealth" as targets, yet it is less able to pinpoint them as individuals and identify them by name today than in the days when Carnegie, Rockefeller, and J. P. Morgan were virtually swearwords. Individual fortunes no longer seem as predatory as they once did. The name of Ford is probably more offensive to those who connect it with the dangerous radicalism of foundation research than to those for whom it connotes grinding the faces of the poor. The Kennedy family have been thought of less as millionaires than as potential leaders of the revolution of youth.

In any case, it is not individual fortunes but the aggregations of wealth, particularly in the great corporations, that consitute the structure of economic power and may be targeted as "capitalism." The great oil companies, General Motors, IBM, the giant industries and banks, monopolistic utilities like the American Telephone & Telegraph Company, vertical oligopolies and horizontal conglomerates whose fortunes hundreds of thousands of investors follow in the stock market reports—these dominate the American economy. Interconnecting empires of publishing and broadcasting dominate the American cultural and intellectual world. Corporate business and finance are intimately interwoven with government at all levels, and corporate executives and their lawyers and friends become governors, senators, cabinet officers, and Presidents. With the vast expansion of the arms industries during World War II and the subsequent Cold War, the monstrous juggernaut of the military-industrial complex has given new shape and coherence to the power of corporate wealth in the United States.

Yet when the would-be revolutionist tries to focus on his target, and, from ghetto cellar or from college library, to identify the enemy as a social class to be overthrown and replaced by another, he may well be baffled. There are, to be sure, rich and powerful people in the United States whose decisions, often without accountability to anyone else, may determine the destiny of millions of their fellow citizens and perhaps the fate of the country itself. They may deal on intimate terms with generals, admirals, scientists, university presidents, newspaper and magazine publishers, cardinals, and occasionally even overlords of organized crime. But how are they to be characterized? They are less capitalists than managers, for their power comes more from management than ownership of capital. The capital they control may be more public than private. Who, after all, owns an Apollo spacecraft?

Some of the literature of the New Left identifies the "technocrats" as the enemy. The word was coined a half-century ago by followers of Thorstein Veblen, but his book *The Engineers and the Price System* pictured the engineers not as powerful but as oppressed, frustrated by a market economy which required that they cut back production to what people could buy, rather than producing the abundance of which their technology was capable. In the Great Depression a movement known as Technocracy proposed that the engineers throw out the politicians, take over the country, and release its productive capacity.

However frustrated engineers might have been in the 1930's, arms production for World War II, the Cold War, Korea, and Vietnam unleashed their machines, and with the weapons came an avalanche of consumer goods.

It might seem as if the engineers had come into their own. Engineering is concerned not only with machines but with management: combining men and machines, as interchangeable units, in systems and processes. Did the new class of technical-managerial bureaucrats get their revolution after all? Perhaps it was what some called the managerial revolution. Have these latter day technocrats, then, become the new ruling class? If so, it is hard to see how these technocrats of the new managerial class are to be differentiated from their middle-class neighbors in the suburbs or from their sons and daughters now restive on the campuses.

And it is hard to fit a man like Robert McNamara into the role of a Nicholas II to be shot in a cellar, or a Louis XVI rolling in a tumbril on the way to the guillotine. McNamara of the Harvard Business School and the Ford Motor Company, the superman of the military-industrial bureaucracy, left the Pentagon ultimately more a victim of forces beyond his control than a wielder of power. Now at the World Bank, he is as much an international civil servant as U Thant.

Our society is so complex, so fluid, with so many and such rapidly shifting centers of decision making, of economic and social power, that identification of its ruling class is anything but easy. Where then is the power structure? Where is the ruling class?

If the young radicals have found no clear answers, this has not held them back. They have tended to believe more in action than in theory. And in action they have often found what to them has seemed an adequate identification of power: bluntly, a policeman's club. They are concerned with the question of when and how that power can be seized and given to a "liberated" people.

Obviously revolutions do not occur when things are going well. Just how bad would things have to become to make a revolution conceivable in the United States?

Mobs have been rampaging, looting, and burning in the heart of our great cities. Crimes of violence have mounted to make city streets and parks unsafe throughout the country. Drug addiction, and the demoralization and crime that go with it, have spread from slums to suburbs and the small towns of America. Schoolteachers and other public servants have introduced the methods of industrial conflict to white collar and professional occupations. Pollution and waste and violence have spread from ungovernable cities to the countryside. Moralists can see a breakdown of discipline, a disintegration of the social order, a failure of nerve on the part of the very people who have built America. And now, despite all our panoply of power, we are unable to defeat a small Asian country that defied us.

Some see a revolutionary situation developing out of the Vietnam fiasco, the mounting disorder, and the collapse of confidence on the part of those holding power. Those who believe a revolution would open the way to something better may try to hasten its coming by promoting and fostering disruptive tendencies in the hope of a break-down into general anarchy. Some are resorting to the traditional anarchist technique of planting bombs.

For all our troubles, we are still a long way from a breakdown now. But if the Vietnam war continues indecisively, if violence continues to grow in the ghetto and on the campus, if peace demonstrations become more violent and the backlash of the frightened middle class becomes more than a fringe reaction, if a rapid increase in unemployment or an increasingly runaway inflation rises to panic proportions, and if these lead to an epidemic of strikes by police, firemen, public utility workers, transportation workers and the like, one can conceive of our delicately balanced economic and technological system reaching a stage more nearly approaching total breakdown. The trigger might be a failure of the distribution of food, with a panicky fear of starvation sweeping city populations.

Such conditions would come quickly in a nuclear war. Even one atom bomb on New York City, the nerve center of trade and finance, could shatter the country's distributive system. Even a minimal nuclear exchange could paralyze the country's power grid and communications network. What happens to law and order, as desperate city dwellers invade the suburbs and clash with Minute Men and vigilantes, as police and National Guard units disintegrate, as the only rule becomes every man for himself?

In such a setting, a disciplined revolutionary organization, knowing what it wanted and prepared to impose its will, might conceivably be able to control chaos and make a revolution. But, as many have predicted, a nuclear war is more likely to return civilization to a new dark age, if it does not wipe out human life entirely. Not even the most fanatical of the New Left have proposed that the ultimate violence is the way to achieve a better social order.

If nuclear war is ruled out, a total breakdown of discipline and order, the kind of disintegration that gave the Bolsheviks their chance in Russia in 1917, seems most improbable. The ability of organized society to carry on even under extreme stress was demonstrated at the end of World War II, when many of the world's great cities lay in ruins, and once rich farm lands swarmed with hungry refugees.

Modern society has many centers of power. It is flexible and adaptable, and can meet crises when and where they occur. Even without basic reform, it is so conditioned to continuous change that it can bend in many directions without breaking. The Russian analogy may be misleading. Power was already in the streets when the Bolsheviks picked it up in 1917, and there was no substantial white collar and suburban middle class able to step in between a collapsing monarchy and the workers and peasants.

Moreover, the American federal system presents special difficulties for those who think in terms of a revolutionary seizure of power in the streets of the capital. We have fifty state capitals in addition to Washington, and dozens of great industrial cities. A revolutionary party would have to seize power in one of those after another, under all sorts of differing circumstances.

To be sure, such a party could perhaps win individual states through the electoral process, during a period of mounting tension. Huey Long's power in Louisiana during the tumultuous 1930's rested on the ballot, and it is possible that his demagogic "every man a king" offensive against established ways would have spread to other states, and even become nationwide, if he had not been assassinated. But New Deal measures and growing military expenditures had already begun to restore the American economy. Long's strength lay with the rednecks, poor farmers and the small town middle-class folk, and if he had led a national revolution it would probably have been more nearly patterned on that of Hitler than of any other. But his following was always more sectional than national.

To attempt to predict how power might be seized by a revolutionary party in this country is to indulge in fantasy. But to see the present New Left, relying on a coalition of student radicals and militant blacks, coming out on top in a time of general breakdown is even more fanciful. American society being what it is, any scramble for power in such a breakdown would give every advantage to the military-technical-managerial classes, supported by the police and the worst racist elements of white suburbia, now typified by the John Birchers and the Minute Men. These elements could probably count on a mass base, as did the Fascist and Nazi movements a half-century ago in Europe.

Some of the more desperate young blacks in the ghetto, and some of the more militant of the white extremists, even when they recognize the danger of a fascist reaction, are willing to take the risk.

They can argue that the urban masses, in a time of breakdown, would join them. They can argue that with the population polarized, the military leadership would be unable to count on the armed forces, which would mutiny if ordered against their own people. Even without such mutiny, they can point to the inability of vastly superior armed might to crush "liberation movements" in Algeria and Vietnam and to prevent prolonged guerrilla warfare.

It is the extreme militants who have sometimes attracted the most attention on TV screens because they have been the most violent. On campuses they have taken over administration offices, vandalized libraries, seized podiums and microphones at public meetings to prevent conservatives or moderates from being heard, and sought to justify such actions as a necessary process of radicalization in preparation for an inevitably violent revolution. In the ghettos they have thrown molotov cocktails and have stocked arms and ammunition for a struggle which they believe will usher in the revolution, though it may cost them their lives. Advocates of peace and universal human brotherhood have sometimes violently disrupted domestic peace, vilified and abused their opponents as less than human, and defied all organized society in the belief that this would hasten the coming of a new day.

If, in a welter of violence, the revolution they hope for ever comes —either as a result of their efforts or as a reaction to their efforts— it would be a time of unimaginable suffering and of destruction of human values. Whoever seized power, whether they called themselves communists, fascists, or liberators, or the forces of law and order, would have to be ruthless in dealing with their opposition. Whatever its professed goals, the outcome of a violent revolution in America today is not likely to resemble what any of those who hoped for it had in mind.

9 | When Is Violence Legitimate?

The radical movements of the turbulent 1960's all started as revolts *against* violence. The black revolt was against a system of white domination maintained by force of law and custom: legal violence for the most part, but violence nonetheless. The cultural and campus revolts of the young were against a society organized for war, a society in which corporate enterprise and scientific research alike seemed to be focused on the art of killing.

Yet by the end of the decade the ideal of non-violence, which had given a special moral force to both the civil rights and the peace movements, had been abandoned by many of the more radical leaders. They had come to believe that the evils they opposed were inherent in a social order which had been built and maintained by violence, and that the system could therefore be changed only by violence. This belief seemed confirmed as the bloodshed continued in Vietnam, and the police clubbed demonstrators and shot it out with the Black Panthers.

Meanwhile riots, assassinations, and mounting crime alarmed politicians and public. By 1968 an epidemic of violence seemed to be sweeping the country. The National Commission on the Causes and Prevention of Violence probed the body politic to determine whether America's illness was fatal. It promptly dispelled the notion that vio-

113

lence was something new or that it was peculiar to this country, but it did find plenty of cause for concern. Among other disquieting facts, it reported that purchases of handguns by private householders, presumably as protection against violent crime and possible mob violence, had doubled, then doubled again, in a decade.

Are we really against violence, or only some violence? And what do people mean by violence?

Traditional attitudes toward violence are full of paradox. The followers of the Prince of Peace, who taught a gospel of love even for enemies but also declared that he brought not peace but a sword, have justified centuries of bloodshed in the name of Christianity. The sword is an accepted symbol not only of courage but of justice. The God of our fathers punished human weakness in a hell whose torments were beyond imagining. With such a cultural background, it is not surprising if many a permissive parent today wonders guiltily whether, in sparing the rod, he has made his child an anarchist.

Yet the religious and secular ideal of western civilization, and particularly of the democratic and egalitarian movements of the last two hundred years, is the worth of the individual human being. All contemporary societies, both those which stress "free enterprise" and those which call themselves "socialist," profess to believe in the same ultimate value. If that is the foundation of morals, then "Thou shalt not kill" is a universal moral imperative, and any violence against another human being, any injury or threat of injury, is immoral.

Violence and gentleness are both built-in components of human nature. To explain man's violence, it is not necessary to picture him, as some social scientists have done, as a peculiarly aggressive animal. But he has had to compete with other animals for space and food. He is still a carnivore and often a hunter. At the same time he has had to be gentle. Like others of the higher animals he has had to care for his young, and his success in the evolutionary struggle has depended on his ability to cooperate harmoniously with his fellow men.

Again, man's survival as a social animal has depended on the ability of his group to survive, and the social group has often invoked group violence in its own struggle for survival. At the group level, however, survival is threatened not only by external enemies, but by internal disruption. Whether the propensity to individual violence be considered a normal human trait or an aberration, it cannot be tolerated by the group beyond a certain point.

Moreover, since any society is complex and there are smaller groupings within any larger one, the larger invokes force to defend itself against disruption not only by the aberrant individual but by the dissident sub-group.

Every organized group depends on law and order founded on force. Behind the judge deciding a dispute stands the sheriff, ready to see that the judge's decision is carried out. Even a voluntary association, whose rules of procedure are consented to by its members, must have means to enforce those rules. The gavel wielded by the chairman of a debating society in applying Robert's *Rules of Order* is not unrelated to the club wielded by a tribal chieftain. The jeweled mace resting in front of the Speaker's chair in the House of Commons is a bludgeon representing the physical force on which any authority ultimately depends.

A chairman may have a special enforcement officer at hand, a sergeant-at-arms, bailiff, doorkeeper or "bouncer," to take care of disruption, but if not he can summon the police.

In most social groups, however, most of the time, authority rests on consent, and force is not needed. Man is governed by habit far more than by either persuasion or compulsion, and most societies are traditional. Some great civilizations have remained static and relatively unchanged for hundreds, even thousands, of years. But the modern world is subject to constant innovation. The law and order of one generation may be the tyranny of the next.

Thomas Jefferson believed that a revolution every thirty years might be necessary if freedom is to survive: the tree of liberty, he said, might need to be periodically watered with blood. Many a liberal today, while deploring violence, has occasionally wondered whether Jefferson was right. Many an advocate of non-violence, recalling the Boston Tea Party, the "shot heard round the world" at Concord Bridge, and Washington crossing the Delaware on Christmas Eve to surprise and slaughter celebrating Hessian mercenaries, has been disturbed by the thought that America might never have become a "sweet land of liberty" if Americans had not been willing to kill and be killed—or at least to seize a private cargo of tea and destroy it. Is eternal violence, then, rather than vigilance, the price of freedom? Can a society be assured of growth and change only by violence?

Violence begets violence, and today's violence is in no small degree the heritage of our violent past. If we would prove Jefferson wrong, we need a social order that, while strong enough to withstand disintegration into anarchy, is also flexible enough to permit continuing change.

The issue is far more difficult today than in Jefferson's time. With the entire human race now a single social group on the face of a shrinking globe, any call to arms for group defense or assertion of group demands may endanger the survival of the whole species. At the same time the pace of social change has so accelerated that undue resistance to new group demands, or rigidity in accommodating to changing circumstances, can quickly build social pressures to the explosive point.

Much depends on whether, when force is invoked, it is felt to be legitimate, and by whom. Almost inevitably force will seem legitimate to the authorities invoking it, but to those against whom it is invoked it will seem illegitimate, and they will call it violence.

The white citizen in suburbia may call for more police protection and stricter law enforcement. To him law and order mean the defense of his home and family. To the black resident of the ghetto the police have too often seemed to be harassing rather than protecting him, and law and order have been synonymous with oppression.

Marx and his followers stated that under the capitalist system the capitalists as a ruling class maintained their power by means of the coercive apparatus of the state, applied in the first instance by the police and the courts and ultimately by the army. After the revolution and the final establishment of a socialist system, they said, the state would wither away, and there would be no further need for the use of force except to restrain the mentally ill and the incorrigible criminal. Yet, fifty years after the Bolshevik revolution, the Soviet Union and the other communist states, all dedicated to the liberation of man, are police states with standing armies ready to reinforce the police.

Regardless of the economic system, the law is what those in power declare it to be, and force is legally used to back it up. To those who feel the social order is theirs, by virtue of their power or their consent or their acceptance of the inevitable, the use of force to compel observance of the law and the maintenance of order is legitimate. Those who feel outside the group, those who do not recognize it as their own, may well feel such use of force illegitimate.

The distinction between force and violence can be made in various ways and is sometimes arbitrary. Violence may simply mean excessive force, more force than reasonably necessary to achieve the result intended. Or it may mean illegitimate force, force used by an authority not recognized, or for a purpose considered unjust or immoral. In either case the distinction is subjective: it depends on who is evaluating the reasonable necessity or the legitimacy of the use of force. If policemen beat a long-haired militant into unconsciousness while breaking up a peace demonstration, they may claim that they used only such force as was necessary to make an arrest, while an objective outsider would see it as excessive force and therefore violence, and the demonstrator would consider the entire police action, even with respect to those not roughly handled, as police violence.

It is not surprising if public officials charged with law enforcement and responsible for the maintenance of order condemn only the actions of peace demonstrations, campus confrontations, and ghetto riots as violent, while their opponents focus on the violence of the police. It is also natural for an older generation, even when holding liberal views, to chide the young for resorting to illegal acts that end in violence when, as the elders view it, peaceful and legal means are available to bring about the changes they desire. Of course it is this basic premise which is challenged by many of the dissident young. According to them, violence or other drastic action is necessary precisely because the needed changes cannot be effectuated otherwise.

The older liberal may point to the fact that, for all their limitations, the traditional forms of democracy in America and western Europe have demonstrated remarkable adaptability to social changes. Many of the reforms advocated by radicals in the last hundred years—public education, health insurance, old age pensions, income taxation, and the like—were enacted, in western Europe and the United States, by relatively conservative governments.

The United States Constitution and the constitutions of all the western democracies provide various devices for facilitating change, not least of which is the freedom to protest and demand change. Freedom of speech and press, and the rights of petition and assembly, now set forth in our own and other Bills of Rights, were originally won by violent revolution. When they were extended in more recent times to industry, it was only after violent struggles that the right to strike and picket and to organize unions was finally recognized as an extension of basic democratic principles. Yet, in each case, the ultimate result of extending legal sanction to these devices for social change was to lessen the need for violence.

Why then the violence of protest today? Part of the explanation lies in the use of the technique of civil disobedience.

The turbulence of the 1960's was ushered in when the laws establishing racial segregation in the Southern states were deliberately violated. Courageous young people staged Freedom Rides in buses and sat in segregated lunchrooms, despite legal penalties and sometimes police or mob violence. In disobeying state laws and local ordinances in the Southern states they were appealing to a higher law, in this case the Federal Constitution, and they succeeded in effecting significant social change.

The early civil rights movements condemned violence, and participants offered no resistance when arrested or when violence was used against them. By the end of the decade, however, as new protest movements on campuses and against the war gained momentum, seizure of buildings and other overt violence signified defiance not merely of laws considered unconstitutional or immoral, but of authority in general. Some radical youths had moved from individual acts of non-violent civil disobedience of bad laws all the way to a program of violent insurrection against the whole legal and social order.

In disobeying a law believed unjust, it may be difficult to avoid breaking other laws which may be valid and necessary. Black students asking to be served in a segregated lunchroom immediately found themselves charged with trespass, and with resisting an officer when they refused to leave. Martin Luther King, denied parade permits for civil rights demonstrations, marched anyway, and was arrested for violations of possibly valid regulations governing the use of streets. The conservative and the timid point out, with some justification, that disobedience of laws considered bad may contribute to a general breakdown of respect for law and hence an increase in crime. Social protest can foster an anarchic attitude that sanctions any lawbreaking if profitable and safe. Since the first looting of stores in ghetto riots, and the first campus rebellions, shoplifting has skyrocketed, and there may be a cause-and-effect relationship.

During the Prohibition era millions of otherwise law-abiding Americans patronized bootleggers and speakeasies, for they believed that the Prohibition law, whatever its moral justification, was unwise and should be repealed. Today millions of Americans feel the same way about the prohibition of marijuana and the tendency to equate all mind-changing drugs with addictive narcotics. Probably one reason for the widespread use of marijuana is protest, including protest against what the young regard as absurd laws. And to a degree these many acts of individual civil disobedience may be said to be succeeding: the disproportionate penalties for possession of marijuana are in the process of being reduced.

Yet this is a kind of civil disobedience where the social cost seems clearly to outweigh the possible gains. Just how harmful marijuana is when regularly used, and to what degree it leads directly to the use of hard drugs, are debatable questions. On the other hand, there is no question at all about the relationship of heroin to street crime, and there seems little question that the expansion of the illegal traffic in marijuana is bound up with the expansion of the narcotics trade. Also, when habitual "pot" smokers are deprived of their supply, as many were after the Nixon Administration's Operation Intercept sharply reduced the illegal importation of marijuana from Mexico, the use of more dangerous drugs increases.

Whatever the impact of widespread civil disobedience on the mores of the time, no one can deny that it is strong medicine. No matter how non-violent the intent, it is never wholly free from an element of violence. Any violation of law is a challenge to those charged with law enforcement; unless ignored, it provokes—and achieves its purpose by provoking—the police to move in, to make an arrest, and to use at least the minimal force required to make an arrest. To the person arrested and any who sympathize with him, this use of force is illegitimate, even if legal and disciplined.

History is full of martyrs, and social upheaval is stimulated by a willingness on the part of the dedicated to suffer for their beliefs. Their suffering may itself be an effective means of winning sympathy and support, and breaking down the resistance of those in authority. Even self-inflicted violence in the form of suicide can be an effective political instrument, as the Buddhist priests in South Vietnam who set themselves on fire so vividly demonstrated when they helped to bring the Diem regime to an end.

Martyrdom aside, the purpose of civil disobedience is more often reformist than revolutionary. It is aimed at achieving a specific action or at the elimination of specific rules which, though still part of the body of law, have lost their legitimacy in the eyes of many besides the protesters. Yet by a natural progression, civil disobedience may come to seem revolutionary both to the participants and to the authorities they defy.

Students fresh from breaking Jim Crow laws in the South occupied university buildings at Berkeley. Some of their less discriminating or more unstable followers went on to vandalism and even arson. Non-violence escalated into incidents of mindless violence.

To the extent that those undertaking civil disobedience are willing to submit to arrest, or to offer only passive resistance to law enforcement authorities, the violence may remain symbolic. Yet even passive resistance may lead to police violence.

Once demonstrators have given up the effort to remain non-violent, and have indicated a willingness to defend themselves and then to provoke violence as a means of heightening the confrontation, civil disobedience has gone a long way toward violent insurrection. That, of course, is now the intent of the most radical.

It was no doubt with this progression in mind that the National Commission on the Causes and Prevention of Violence came to a painful division of opinion in its conclusions on civil disobedience. The black and the more liberal members of the commission pointed to the social gains achieved in the civil rights movement by massive civil disobedience, and felt the results were worth the cost. A bare majority of the commission felt otherwise, and opposed any but individual acts of civil disobedience aimed at a law that is felt beyond question to be morally repugnant.

Civil disobedience may be morally justifiable; in fact at times it may be a moral imperative. But the social costs may outweigh the gains. Like fire, it can be useful, but like fire, it is always dangerous.

Yet if the good citizen thinks he can avoid violence by obeying the law, he may be no less a party to it, at least in the eyes of the person who views the law as unjust or evil. Silence, too, can be a crime. Those Germans who did nothing to oppose Hitler, however little they may have sympathized with the extermination of the Jews, share some of the guilt of the Nazis. Those who have disapproved of the war in Vietnam, but have done nothing to prevent or end it, share some of the guilt of My Lai.

These are times that try men's consciences. Many thoughtful minds of the older generation as well as of the young, conservatives no less than liberals and radicals, those with a measure of power and those seeking power, are torn today over the issue of violence. Revolted by violence, they nevertheless cannot exorcize the arguments that seem to justify it.

Morally, all may agree, violence denies another person freedom of action and negates his essential human quality. Yet freedom has been won and human dignity preserved by those willing to do battle for them.

Violence is the negation of democracy, for it prevents the reasoned communication and tolerance which are essential to participation in decision-making. Yet there would have been no democratic institutions without armed struggle against traditional despotisms. Clearly the issue is one of ends and means.

No rational person would claim that violence is an end in itself. Warped individuals, to be sure, may enjoy the infliction of pain, and a genuine blood-lust associated with sexual excitement may be the mark of a few pathological killers. Under stress, or under the influence of drugs, disturbed individuals may infect others with sadistic impulses, and even relatively normal individuals may become habituated to cruelty or make a cult of evil. Such abnormalities were undoubtedly a factor in the atrocities of Buchenwald and Auschwitz, and may help to explain bizarre cults like the motorcycle gangs. But violence for its own sake is not normally what the violent are after.

Even those who glorify war do so for other ends—national greatness or a dream of freedom for a people or for all mankind. Those young Americans who now take Mao and Che Guevara as their heroes, and make a fetish of the gun, extol the same virtues of courage and sacrifice as the militarist, but they claim a unique vision of a world of peace and harmony beyond the violence.

There is no doubt that war makes heroes, and inspires many with a higher moral purpose than does an enervating peace. There is no doubt that armed revolt against oppression can liberate as well as kill.

Even acts of vandalism and terrorism may give self-confidence and pride to people long humiliated or crushed by foreign rule. The example of the Algerian revolt against French colonial rule, marked by savagery on both sides, is cited by those who would rouse the downtrodden to revolt. The S.D.S. no longer demands simply peace in Vietnam but calls upon fighting men to "bring the war home." People long oppressed may no doubt regain something of lost manhood when they take up the sword—or rather its modern equivalent, the fire bomb—to confront their oppressors.

Furthermore, some of the attitudes that make for democracy may be developed in the process of fighting. Even in a setting of military discipline, the sense of brotherhood, of belonging to an organized group, identification with the combat unit, cooperation in a common struggle, can provide experience in participation and even a kind of responsible citizenship. To the extent that the struggle is entered into voluntarily, and not in defense of an imposed social order, it may promote the development of democratic ways. What may look like a mob or start out as a mob, such as a group of workers on strike, may well develop new and democratic forms of social organization in the process of fighting a common enemy.

Yet these gains from the appeal to violence are all secondary. The growth of democratic procedures was in response to the need to organize, for battle or a strike, rather than as outcome of the battle itself. The sense of identification with a cause greater than oneself comes from engaging in a common enterprise, not necessarily a violent one. Physical courage and collective loyalty can be fostered no less on a football field than on a battlefield.

And over against possible benefits from the use of violence stand its costs. It brutalizes even when it redeems. It hurts the man of violence, whether private citizen, soldier or policeman, no less than his victim. His reason—the essential quality of "homo sapiens"—is debased. As the adrenalin is pumped into his system, riotous student as well as policeman may become a "fascist pig." As Nietzsche put it, "Those who set out to kill monsters should take care not to turn into monsters themselves."

Mass violence, whether of the mob or of a disciplined army, whether aimed at conquest or liberation, destroys not only the lives and livelihood and cultural heritage of its victims but the very state of mind—tolerance, civility, and mutual respect—which constitutes a social environment favorable to democracy. Even if armies are not aimed at imperial conquest or repression but come as liberators, they become oppressors in their turn. If armed rebels are too weak to achieve their liberating goal but merely threaten their oppressors, the backlash, the reaction, the counterrevolution, will intensify the oppression. If premature, an insurrection may indefinitely delay the liberation hoped for.

Moreover, behind the appeal to violent revolution, however remote the likelihood of its taking place and even more remote its success, stands the menace of the ultimate violence. The doomsday machine is not a mere figure of speech or a science fiction nightmare. Unrestrained and indiscriminate violence could end the human adventure with no one left to write its history. Those who advocate violence today, whether military men who accept war as a natural human activity, or revolutionists who believe a violent transfer of power to be the only method of social change, are placing their faith in violence at a time when the ultimate violence means mass suicide. Seen from the moon, the Kremlin and the Pentagon may be indistinguishable. Certainly their ruins will look much the same.

Confronted by this awful truth, perhaps establishmentarian and dissident alike can learn the importance of a rational restraint in the use of force, whether in defending our system or confronting it. Even when enraged, most men retain an instinctive sense of the limits to which they may go. In all the tensions and the turmoil of the 1960's —the riots and police violence, the fire bombs and tear gas and dynamite, the increasing use of firearms on both sides—the total loss of life would probably not equal the accident toll on a single holiday weekend, or the body count after a week of intense fighting in Vietnam.

Is it possible that we have in fact been learning what many of the higher animals learned earlier in their evolution, that violence can be controlled and tamed, that it may serve its purpose just as well when only a ritual?

Most of the higher animals seem to play at violence. Lion cubs and kittens, young wolves and puppy dogs wrestle and snarl and pretend to bite. Even mature animals, in a real fight over food or for a mate or for dominance, rarely carry a battle to the finish. The biological urge to release energy in violent play is no less apparent in man, and individual aggression usually finds an outlet without blows.

Much juvenile violence begins with boredom and an urge for excitement, and contains an element of bravado and make-believe. Street gangs tend to have romantic names like Apaches, Rangers, Rovers.

Effective neighborhood workers can sometimes channel energies into basketball or other sports. Many a potential delinquent has been helped to become a useful member of society by a rugged summer camp experience. Students who are able to participate in strenuous competitive sports seem less likely to concern themselves with violent revolution.

Even the contemporary American revolutionists have, for the most part, limited themselves to symbolic violence. The language of obscenity is sometimes a useful ritual in this respect. When physical violence is undertaken, it is generally aimed at property, not persons. Even in the case of the S.D.S. Weathermen who tried to provoke street fighting and charged the police in Chicago in October 1969, the operation looked more like a kind of violent game than a revolutionary skirmish. Some of them even wore football helmets.

Not only has the number of people killed in riots or demonstrations, in the ghetto or on campus, been very small, but serious injury has more often been accidental than intentional. Well-trained police know that a show of force is preferable to its use. In the countries of western Europe, in which the cult of the gun is not so rampant as in America, policemen are seldom armed. Even in the most violence-prone American cities, "kill the pigs" remains a figure of speech, and "guerrilla warfare" a violent phrase for some far less drastic activity.

To the extent that violence remains ritualized in these ways, society has not broken down, and the physical and psychological damage done by violence can by common consent be kept within reasonable limits. Unhappily, violence has a tendency to escalate from the symbolic to the real. Small fire bombs are replaced by lethal charges of dynamite, capable of killing not only their inept makers but innocent bystanders as well. Student protesters, not satisfied with boycotts or building take-overs, find themselves roughing up deans and teachers. In their zeal to oppose militarism with its connotations of self-righteous repression, they ape what they hate in their enemies by howling down speakers and physically preventing class sessions from taking place.

As the symbolic and often verbal violence which now characterizes much of the radical activity fails to achieve its purpose, those who talk of guerrilla warfare and revolution may take their own war cries more seriously. Thus the major confrontations they profess to want may actually come to pass, and the result is almost certain to be tragedy. The kind of methodical slaughter our literal-minded and dedicated military men have been capable of in Vietnam may then become the pattern for the American city and countryside.

Has it already begun? In some cities the Black Panthers and police forces are almost in a shooting war. In August of 1970, a California judge was taken as a hostage in his own courtroom by black inmates from San Quentin prision and shot to death in the ensuing melee; the coup was a failure, as the fleeing prisoners and an accomplice were also killed, but the event, extolled by Panther leaders, gave the rest of the country a sense of slipping back to barbarism.

Just as there has been a dangerous escalation on the side of the protesters, there has been increased violence on the side of the Establishment. During the Democratic National Convention in 1968, the Chicago police killed no one, in spite of all the turmoil. But in May, 1970, within the space of a few days, six students—four white, two black—were shot and killed byNational Guardsmen and State troopers.

Unhappily, a huge group of Americans—perhaps a majority— shared the reported feeling of the townspeople of Kent, Ohio, that the students "had it coming". This was more than polarization; it seemed to represent a new level of fear and hatred of one mass of Americans by another.

Such intensification of hostility is of course welcomed by revolutionaries, who see in it greater opportunities for the major confrontations they seek. But fortunately this is not the usual reaction, even among activists and radicals. The student deaths, coming on top of Nixon's invasion of Cambodia, shocked and angered a whole new segment of hitherto uninvolved Americans, and unprecedented numbers of protesters—not only students and teachers, but lawyers, architects, businessmen—made themselves felt in Washington, determined to change the direction of America. The stubborn refusal of many Senators and Representatives to heed the spreading demands for an end to the Indochina war galvanized a host of young people to for an end to the Indochina war galvanized a host of young people to a new burst of political activity. And the hostility of middle America to the violence-prone demonstrators persuaded many leaders of the anti-war movement that their past tactics had antagonized too many potential allies in the struggle against the war.

Also, fortunately for the future of American democracy, the dominant strain of youthful radicalism in this country, however impulsive, is not violent. It is emotional rather than logical, and in its revolt against modern technology it has downgraded the intellect. Yet despite the symptoms of emotional and mental disturbance some of these young people display, they may be of significant help in restoring our crazy world to sanity. For all their uncouth raucousness and all their make-believe violence, this new generation searching for a new way of life may, almost in spite of themselves, bring a new civility to civilization, a new urbanity to urban life, a new sociability to society.

Part Four

Participatory Democracy

10 | On a Human Scale

When Students for a Democratic Society was organized at Port Huron, Michigan, in 1962, it defined its goal as "a democracy of individual participation". In a statement drafted by Tom Hayden, still a leading figure in the New Left, the S.D.S. called for a social system in which the individual could "share in those social decisions determining the quality and direction of his life".

This remains the clearest statement of the positive goals of a movement which, growing out of protest against things as they are, has often seemed more negative than positive.

Subsequent events tended to obscure the original objectives and methods of the S.D.S. The tough realities of trying to change a social order, the escalation of violence on both domestic and foreign battlefronts, the conflicting claims of the various groups of the restless younger generation, led to disillusionment with the idealistic hope of a non-violent transition to a new democracy expressed in the Port Huron statement. Yet the demand for participation grows out of a deeply felt need. It is bound to find expression and characterize whatever constructive change comes out of this period of turmoil.

Participatory democracy has not caught on as a slogan, perhaps because four-letter words are easier to pronounce. But the concept itself has had a growing impact. The idea of participation was given

131

official sanction in the politically explosive requirement of President Johnson's Economic Opportunity Act, that community action programs in slum neighborhoods must involve the "maximum feasible participation" of the poor themselves. In many, perhaps most, of the O.E.O. programs this requirement remained only a pious hope, but it helped to stimulate some of the most significant and creative expressions of the ghetto revolt. The battles that raged about the decentralized and experimental school districts in New York, in the fall of 1968, also focused attention on the idea of community participation and resulted in greater autonomy for district school boards in the city.

In another major arena of conflict and unrest, the campus, student demands for opportunities to share in the decisions that shape their education have initiated profound changes in university governance.

Yet, for the most part, participatory democracy remains only an expression of a vague desire for positive involvement. Even today it has not been subjected to detailed analysis or set forth in specific programs. It has not even been defined.

Obviously more is involved than definition. Democracy has many meanings, and its meanings have been changing. If content is to be given to the yearnings of a new generation for a participation more substantial than voting on election day, we need to be clearer about what democracy has meant in the past and what it might mean in the future.

Democracy is related in a very fundamental way to the nature of the human being as a social animal. Born of the mating of two, reared in a family, becoming human in the company of others, man can hardly exist in solitude. Psychologists have found that a baby may be provided with all its material needs, but without the warm bodily contact of at least one other member of the species it will not develop as a full human being. The pioneers of ethology, the science of animal behavior, have shown that many of the higher animals, too, depend on patterns of group living, often similar to those of man.

Bisexual reproduction and the helplessness of the human infant make some kind of family grouping inevitable. It may be polygamous, polyandrous or monogamous, it may be more or less extended to include collateral relations, it may be temporary or permanent, shifting or stable, but the basic institution of society is still the family.

Within the family and beyond it, the human being is always both an individual, seeking freedom to express his individuality, enraged by restraint, and at the same time a member of a group, finding his identity in relation to others, learning that his freedom exists in a structure of order and discipline.

He finds the meaning of his existence in the consciousness of belonging. The child belongs to his parents or to a larger family or to some other group, but they also belong to him. He speaks of *my* family, *my* school, *my* gang, and later, often enough, of *my* company and *my* country. Loving and being loved are necessary to each other. A child grows as he takes part in group activity, and as his participation is recognized.

Life and growth are positive and creative activities, and a family, like any other group, flourishes to the extent that it is engaged in creative activity. Begetting and bearing children and being responsible for their maintenance is the basic group activity, but the modern family has learned how fragile and expendable an institution it is when its group activity ends there. For most of man's past history the family was an economic unit, producing and consuming together, sustained by a sense of purpose and meaning. But other social groupings, engaged in collective activities, can provide the same sense of common purposes actively pursued. In isolation, on the other hand, life is sterile and meaningless.

It is, then, in belonging to a group and sharing in its activities that man finds his being. This is what Rebecca West called "the sweetness of conformity to good ends." Only in such participation can a man feel truly at home in the universe.

These observations may seem obvious, but they are relevant to the problems of the world around us. The disintegration of the family in industrial society, particularly in the present urban slum and ghetto, is a major source of mental illness, crime and violence. The lack of active involvement of children in purposeful family and community activities has much to do with juvenile delinquency, and contributes to the despair and alienation with which many even of the most favored young people look on the world around them.

In the past the feeling of being identified with and belonging to a large group in whose activities and purposes we may share has tended to be strongest with respect to our country. Patriotism has been a kind of religion, and its symbols and rituals have been endowed with special meaning.

One of the reasons for the acute disaffection of the young rebels of today is that the war in Vietnam has destroyed their faith in their country: the institutions of political democracy, so painfully developed by their ancestors, but no longer offering them a meaningful sense of participation, could not hold their loyalty. At the same time many other groupings, economic and social, public and private, which might have given them the sense of belonging, had acquired a common forbidding bureaucratic character, huge, dehumanized, and impersonal.

The democracy sought by the young is more than a form of government. It is a principle of collective human effort. It would reconcile the values cherished by the individual with the values sought by the social group. It would enable the individual to fulfill himself in the group activities that comprise society.

As so conceived, it is clear that democracy has survival value. Any group organized in such a way as to enlist the full participation of all its members—their emotional loyalty no less than their physical and mental capacities—will have a competitive advantage. To the extent that labor may be considered free it is more productive than slave labor. To the extent that the countries of western Europe and North America have achieved political democracy, they have had an advantage when challenged by totalitarian dictatorship.

Political democracy, it was earlier suggested, put primary emphasis on liberty, while social democracy emphasized equality. The present phase of the democratic revolution gives most weight to the third element of the old revolutionary slogan: fraternity. To the extent that participatory democracy can realize that ideal, the prospect for human survival will be enhanced.

Rebellious youth is, of course, clearer on what it is against than on what it is for. In turning against a society which seemed to make a mockery of human brotherhood the evils of war and racism were clear enough. But the more complex and subtle problem of restoring an organic relationship between the individual and society was attacked only gropingly.

The "flower children," whose sensitivity if not their urge to action was enhanced by the new drugs, first scrawled "Make love not war" as their contribution to revolutionary slogans. But their withdrawal from the world was no answer even to their own sense of alienation. Many of them recognized that love was more than sexual pairing and found expression in creative group endeavor, in community activity, but they found it difficult to maintain the principle of everyone being free to "do their thing," working or freaking out, as the mood struck them. Love, like freedom, needs structure, even discipline for its fullest realization.

Those radicals who became activists in a struggle against the "system" gave freely of themselves, and found a measure of personal fulfillment in working with others, against the war, against racial prejudice, against corporate power. But as they made a romantic cult of revolution and adopted a pose of revolutionary violence, whatever the justification—and in the case of the black revolt it was not hard to find justification—they often became as reckless of human values as the militarists and police "pigs" whom they targeted as enemies.

The satisfactions of participatory democracy unfortunately do not depend on the validity of a group's aims. A mob, whether a lynch mob or a police mob, a revolutionary mob or a counter-revolutionary mob, can bring out the worst in human nature, while at the same time giving the participants the glow of sharing in a crusade. The morale of any organized group, whether a special forces unit on an extermination mission in Vietnam, or an industrial plant manufacturing nuclear weapons, depends on the extent to which the individual participant identifies with the group and feels its aims are his. The militant Weathermen of the S.D.S. who have turned from phrasemaking to making bombs have no doubt learned something of the meaning of participatory democracy even if their methods would deny it to all others.

However, the vast majority of youthful rebels today are neither reckless nor irresponsible. Despite the scorn with which they sometimes speak of liberals, they have not abandoned the liberal creed that every human being is worth consideration. If they are seeking, consciously or unconsciously, for a society in which they can play a significant role, they want to assure everybody the same opportunity.

Yet they are Utopians without a Utopia. Earlier generations of radicals had an ideal society in view: they called it Socialism or the Cooperative Commonwealth or even Communism, and they were not afraid of centralized power to plan and direct the social process for the common good. The young radicals of today know that centralized power is their enemy, even though they may despair of finding an alternative.

Despair drives some into a romantic anarchism, prepared to destroy all the structures and disciplines of an over-organized society in the naïve hope that a freer society, in which men would voluntarily cooperate without imposed disicipline, would somehow emerge. Others seek escape from what they feel is the inevitable tyranny of the large organization required by modern technology, and try to create a new kind of group existence in primitive settlements on the edge of the wilderness. Their enthusiasm for communes stems partly from their awareness that the smaller the group the more chance there is for the individual to find significance through active participation in it.

The success of the *kibbutzim* in Israel has revived the urge, not felt in America since the nineteenth century, to try to build a perfect society in miniature. The self-help colony or collective of today may be no closer to utopia than was Hawthorne's Brook Farm. At best it is not likely to do more than produce some of its own food, and perhaps some simple manufactured article for cash income. But it can give the member a comforting sense of individual and personal involvement.

Yet, obviously, modern civilization depends on the large enterprise. A commune can only make believe that it is supplying its needs with its own efforts and its own resources. The hippie, whether spending a quarterly check from the "square" world he left or perhaps panhandling or shoplifting to make both ends meet, and wanting electric power even for his music, is still dependent on the system, with its giant machines and giant organizations.

The effort to simplify life appeals to many who have no desire to live in a commune but are increasingly aware of the threats to our environment carried by an economy geared to maximizing consumption. The sense of oppression, of being tyrannized over by the impersonal giants of American corporate business, springs in part from a sense of our helplessness as consumers.

Yet few of us have any inclination to be active participants in those many collective activities which concern us as consumers. The militant activist demonstrating against the system, no less than the most disengaged hippie, welcomes the automatic and computerized matrix of public services and conveniences, the telephone, the postal system, expressways, the monetary and banking system, and would seldom want to bother with decisions on how they should be run.

The open market is the only practical mechanism whereby the individual as consumer can participate in the economic system. His freedom of choice is continually threatened by monopoly, whether natural or artificial, and by the manipulations of the hucksters of Madison Avenue.

All the anti-trust laws, regulatory agencies and other safeguards of the freedom of the market place devised by earlier generations of liberals and radicals are still needed, and a constant battle must be waged to maintain and strengthen them, and to devise new techniques of consumer protection if we are not to be helpless victims of greed, irresponsibility and bureaucratic unconcern. One of the most appealing figures in the present revolt against the huge impersonal corporation is that champion of the consumer, Ralph Nader: a modern David challenging Goliath, he became a symbol of what one man could do against the greatest of the corporate giants.

However, it was not on behalf of the consumer that the slogan of participatory democracy was raised. Rather, it was on behalf of the citizen and the employee. In Dustin Hoffman's famous movie, the prospect of a job in a company producing plastics, as the great reward for success in college, drove the Graduate to furious if erratic revolt. Leaving aside the question whether plastics are relevant to civilization —and they may now be as basic to our technology as metals—the question troubling many a graduate is how he can remain human if he becomes part of a huge corporate enterprise. How can he share in those decisions that will determine the "quality and direction of his life"? In what kind of a job can he gain the feeling of personal significance that comes with participation in a common effort for a common end that he believes worthwhile?

Participation can be most emotionally satisfying in its simplest and most elemental form, muscle power. When neighbors in a New England village got together to raise the frame of a new barn, they provided a classic example of community enterprise. Some of the hippie colonies today have that nostalgic picture in mind. Nothing gives an individual as much sense of his participation in a group, and gives the group as much sense of its collective identity, as a common physical task to which all bend their backs.

Most group activities, of course, depend on far more specialization of function than does a barn raising. Yet an individual can enjoy the same sense of lending a hand when he contributes special knowledge or skill, along with others' different but comparable contributions. But only if the common undertaking is understood and accepted. If the ultimate products to which he devotes his energies are remote and only vaguely apprehended if at all, the work will seem meaningless and the worker will feel alienated.

Not only must the worker understand and value the ultimate product if he is to get satisfaction from his work, but he must also be able to apply his skill and knowledge and creativity. Nothing made the industrial revolution more dreadful to millions of its victims than the deadly monotony of mechanical operations. Fortunately the new technology has reversed that trend: as mechanical work is taken over by automation and unskilled labor is eliminated, opportunities appear for the more rewarding work of the technician and engineer.

How to give every participant in a vast enterprise the opportunity to be creative is a major challenge confronting the science of management. Industrial plants have long had suggestion boxes. Some offer rewards for innovations and inventions. It has often been noted that the productivity of employees rises when they take part in a pilot project, for then, often for the first time, they have the feeling of doing something creative. Research and development, now usually limited to a separate department in an enterprise, should be open to all the creative imagination available.

Potentially, modern technology can exalt the individual person rather than reducing him to a number in a computer. Even war no longer has any use for the phalanx, for masses of men moving in unison. Automation in industry has meant that machines have taken the place of human automatons. There is no intrinsic reason why a business corporation cannot give even thousands of individuals the feeling of "doing their thing."

Techniques of organization and operation of a large organization can be devised to make it more compatible with the democratic ideal. Equality, obviously, has little to do with it. Inequality is built into the large organization as it is into the smallest, for the simple reason that individuals are different, and when they join in a common task their contributions are different. Even hierarchy is a fact of nature. If democracy is to be defined only in terms of equality of participation —as in the formula "one man, one vote"—it will remain as limited and uninspiring as it seems to many young people today. It need not be so defined.

Whatever an organization's functions, its efficiency will depend on factors of individual and group psychology. The personnel manager of any large business knows that a worker will do better work if his emotions are positively involved, if his significance as a person and the significance of his work are recognized, if he and his fellowworkers develop a personal identification with what they think of as "our" company.

These attitudes may be promoted in ways that have little or nothing to do with the real function of the enterprise or with its direction and control, and the same techniques may be employed in a public as in a private enterprise, under a communist regime no less than under capitalism.

In the Soviet Union, where the need of individual motivation is all the more urgent because of the greater weight of official bureaucracy, every plant has an honor roll, and a scoreboard of achievement records of the individual and working group. Prizes and honorific titles reward the loyal worker, and the incompetent and the bungler are held up to scorn and ridicule. Dances, entertainments, cultural activities and sports clubs tend to give the factory some of the aspects of a genuine community in which all have a share. Large enterprises maintain athletic teams whose intramural and extramural contests arouse the same happy emotions of supporting the team as in the traditional American college.

American enterprises use similar techniques, though with more finesse. Effective management knows the value of having the members of the organization feel they belong. It may be tempted to make a Christmas party a substitute for a raise in pay, and the built-in conflict of interest between the employer and the employee will give any such festivity a quality of hypocrisy. But the sense of being a participant in a common undertaking may still be real enough, and will help to humanize an undertaking that would otherwise be wholly impersonal.

The same may be said for the recently developed device of sensitivity training, introduced by management into many large organizations. The purpose is usually to develop among the executives, in the upper levels of the bureaucratic pyramid, an understanding of the emotional attitudes that get in the way of their working together. Jealousy, timidity, aggressiveness, and prejudice can often be brought to the surface. Some of the same methods are now being applied in community efforts to lessen racial tensions, and in schools and churches to improve understanding among all those involved in their activities.

However effective any of these devices may be, in substituting a mood of friendly cooperation for suppressed grievances and hidden animosities, they can do no more than create the illusion of democracy. Unless one shares in the decisions of the group in which one participates, one is not a free agent and the democracy is incomplete. A company or organization may have the most enlightened management, giving its employees or members the feeling that they belong to a big family, and offering every opportunity for creative work, but if management decisions are made solely by those at the top of a pyramid, no sophisticated participant will be fooled into thinking it truly "his" enterprise.

There was a sure instinct behind the demand of the young radicals for a share in decision-making. So far they have had an opportunity to try their hand at fashioning new techniques of governance only for universities. But all large organizations present similar problems and opportunities to those who want to have a say in what concerns them.

11 | Who Decides What, When and How?

A t one extreme the man at the top of an enterprise makes all the decisions. In most traditional societies the father was the head of the family, and the women, children, and slaves took their orders from him. The authoritarian and hierarchical pattern is still found in all societies and in all kinds of groups. Even in an ideally democratic society some emergency situations will always require the kind of prompt decision-making provided by an absolute dictator.

The master-servant relationship still obtains in many industrial and business organizations, even when the boss plays volleyball with his workers at the annual picnic. But it is as out of style as absolute monarchy.

In western Europe and America it has been replaced by a system of decision-making that has come to resemble the political system, in that it is based on the protection of certain rights and freedoms, and on a balance of power. Constitutional safeguards are set forth in legislation and in union contracts. Some decisions are even subject to majority vote: election of union officials and delegates, balloting to determine collective bargaining agents, election of committees to handle grievances and personnel matters, and to conduct social programs and charity fund drives.

Occasionally more basic issues of management have been handled

143

by representative bodies of workers. In two noteworthy American industries, coal mining and the New York needle trades, unions have at times been in a stronger position than were the relatively weak and unorganized employers, and hence able to take a leading role in formulating policies of investment, mechanization, and marketing, for the whole industry. Other industries have set up profit-sharing plans in which elected representatives of workers are given a say in financial and pricing policies since these directly affect the amount of profit to be shared.

In some countries where socialist ideas have been strong, elected "works councils" have participated in major management decisions. In other countries a "corporative" scheme—once favored by Catholic theorists, but somewhat discredited when Italian Fascists turned it to their own purposes in the 1920's—called for elected representatives of employers, employees, and the public to supervise each industry within a pattern of coordination for all private enterprise. The N.R.A. (National Recovery Administration) of the early New Deal period, declared unconstitutional before it could fairly be tried, was a similar experiment in applying some of the methods of representative democracy to various industries. It tended, however, to foster monopoly and give the advantage to big business.

As recently as 1968 similar proposals were advanced by President De Gaulle, only to be forgotten when he left office shortly thereafter: they were intended to implement his promise to make the still paternalistic French economy more participatory.

Efforts to bring representative democracy into the conduct of industry and business have not been popular with organized labor. The whole history of the labor movement has conditioned it to the idea of union leadership sitting as an adversary across the table from management, not sharing responsibilities with it. Workers do not go on strike to win the right to elect members of the board of directors.

Perhaps disillusionment with the representative techniques of political democracy may help explain lack of interest in trying to use the same methods in the economic system. The procedures by which stockholders pretend to exercise their rights of ownership, in annual elections of corporation directors, hardly inspire employees—some of whom might even be stockholders—to look on electoral democracy as the way to participate in decisions that affect their daily lives. Those same procedures have not been markedly successful in giving workers a sense of participation in running their own unions.

Similar disillusionment has attended efforts to extend representative democracy into the economic system by way of cooperatives. The owners of a cooperative, whether producers pooling their product or consumers pooling their buying power, operate on the principle of "one man, one vote." Yet the bright hopes of enthusiasts who saw this as a democratic alternative to the capitalist system have not been realized. Cooperatives have been successful mainly to the extent that they resemble capitalist businesses, and they have many of the same limitations and frustrations. Their employees confront the management in ways not essentially different from employees in any chain store. Even the voting members are likely to feel as far from the management and its decisions as stockholders in a corporation.

No doubt there is room for innovation and further expansion in the application of the methods of elective and representative democracy to economic enterprise. But the revolutionary demand of the new generation is for direct participation in decision-making by those engaged in any undertaking.

Direct democracy is indeed possible in a small enterprise owned by those who work in it, such as a family farm, or a family owned and operated shop, or a small business partnership in which a group of individuals pool their resources and are collectively self-employed. Similarly, in group medical practice or a law partnership, even though employees outside the partnership have no say in management, those within the group are a self-governing collective. But is even that degree of direct democracy possible in a large enterprise?

Collective ownership was once thought to be essential to industrial democracy. Most socialists and communists left this to a distant future, believing that state or government ownership must come first, while the syndicalist movements—represented in this country by the

I.W.W. (Industrial Workers of the World)—urged workers to seize and operate factories as their collective property from the first moment of the expected revolution.

Only in Yugoslavia have industrial workers retained a significant participation in the control of industrial plants following a socialist revolution. Otherwise, only in agriculture has collective ownership been at all permanent. And only when on a relatively small scale has it been genuinely democratic.

On Soviet collective farms little enough democracy survived the combined pressures of centralized economic planning, the party dictatorship, and the drive for bigness, which for the sake of mechanization resulted in collective farms up to a hundred square miles in extent and with thousands of "members." Most of the communist countries have apparently learned that no type of collective farm in a dictatorship could match the productivity of the individual peasant, who had the direct incentive of personal gain to keep him busy. Only in the liberating atmosphere of Israel has truly collective farming been successful, and this was only on a relatively small scale.

Whether under capitalism or socialism, collective management decisions have generally been possible only in very small enterprises. Nothing better explains the frustrating and alienating quality of life in a highly developed technological society. The individual feels overwhelmed by bigness. The necessity of surrendering imagination and originality for specialized competence is a characteristic not only of big business and industry, but of government and science and learning, and of all the vast institutions that serve human needs and the general welfare.

And so it appears that the chief problem confronting the advocates of participatory democracy is to invent ways of introducing the benefits of smallness into what is big.

This is hardly a new problem. Every big organization already has dealt with it by some kind of decentralization in managerial decision-making. Many have a network of committees and subcommittees, task forces, teams, details, and detachments in which individuals participate—within strict limits, no doubt, but in ways that often lift them out of the humdrum and servile and routine into the excitement of creative innovation.

The smaller the units and sub-units into which any organization is divided, the greater the opportunities for individual participation. For the number of people who can actively share in any decision is always limited. A practical measure of that limit, as long ago noted, is the number who can sit around a table. A task force or committee of five is more effective than one of twelve, and beyond that number real consensus and a genuinely collective decision may have to give way to voting and decision by the majority.

Student radicals have been criticized for not respecting the will of the majority, but their craving for full participation was not to be satisfied by the counting of noses. When in their protests they have seized and occupied university buildings they have often insisted thereafter that all their decisions be by unanimous consent. If the occupying group is large they may argue all night on their demands and their tactics. The result is often near chaos, and those who cannot accept a decision may be summarily ejected.

Yet consensus and unanimity in decision-making are valid goals. The Quakers have long rejected the notion that a decision by majority vote does full justice to the minority. Every gathering of equals, particularly when it is a small board or committee, knows that it is better to arrive at the "sense of the meeting" than to force a vote. Yet the bigger the group the more difficult it becomes to reach a decision to which all have contributed.

The only way a large organization can satisfy the desire of its members for full participation, then, is by breaking down its functions and its structure into bits and pieces. The very complexity and intricacy of economic and governmental and social institutions might, if we had the wit, widen rather than narrow the scope for personal involvement.

The degree of participation possible in a large enterprise varies greatly from one area of management decision to another. Direct involvement of all levels of employees, if found at all, is likely to be limited to off-duty activities. The paternalistic provision of facilities and funds for recreational and social purposes, less popular than it once was, usually permitted employees to run such activities themselves.

Of more direct concern are managerial decisions on the conditions of work in the enterprise. Initially the sole prerogative of management, questions relating to working hours, holidays, shifts, and the health, safety, and comfort of employees are, when not prescribed by law, increasingly subject to collective bargaining. But in a more democratic climate many of them could be left to the direct decisions of those involved.

The same option for wider participation in decision-making might well be provided for other aspects of the working environment: facilities and amenities, from drinking fountains to snack bars and lunchrooms; rules governing behavior on the job; smoking, talking; the courtesies and intangibles that make a shop or office a pleasant place to work or the reverse.

Similarly, though more closely related to the business itself, the physical layout of the plant, the location and expansion of access areas and working areas and their maintenance and policing, parking and traffic control, both outside and inside the plant—all these are matters of daily concern for everyone, as much for the unskilled laborer as the top executive. Most questions of this kind are assumed to be for management to decide, but there is no reason why most of them cannot be decided more democratically, either through collective bargaining, or by joint decision of representatives of all those concerned, or even by direct referendum, in which each man has one vote.

Though such issues may not be directly related to the business itself, they do involve expenditures, and therefore have a bearing on the financial aspects of the business. In a capitalist system a business is run to make a profit for its owners, and they or the managers they employ decide how money is to be obtained or spent. The raising of new capital, investment in expansion, budgeting, are management prerogatives, but they affect everybody connected with the business. Nothing more emphasizes the arbitrary way in which a private enterprise can dispose of the lives of thousands than the decision to close down a plant and move to another location. Major policy decisions affecting the whole business or large parts of it should be subject to the same kind of restraints on arbitrary or irresponsible action as are now found in many areas of government.

Many financial decisions, such as the pricing of products and the purchasing of materials, may be highly technical and may be determined less by human choice than by computers. But the price paid for labor—wage and salary scales and fringe benefits—once wholly under management control, is now the main subject of collective bargaining. Many financial decisions, such as the determination of whether net earnings are to be paid to stockholders as dividends or to go to investment in plant, or to bonuses and higher salaries, are interrelated and affect all those engaged in the business, wage-earners no less than executives. Again, as a general proposition, all those affected by any such decision should have a share in making it.

Yet the traditional democratic method, decision by majority vote, is rarely applicable. The process whereby money is raised or spent by a state or national legislature, also involving highly technical financial operations and affecting the whole economy, may provide a more useful model. Representative legislative and advisory bodies, open hearings, joint committees, lobbies, even political parties or their equivalent, may have their counterparts in a business. Every enterprise is different, and a different pattern might be appropriate to each.

The operation of any industrial or commercial enterprise involves continuous decisions on long-range policies and day-to-day details. Many such decisions must be left to individuals with specialized knowledge and skills. Technical know-how can be found at all levels. The executive with the big salary has authority over subordinates who know more than he does about the specific subject of the orders he gives. The hierarchical pattern has the virtue of simplicity. But if every individual's capacities are to be made full use of, the organization will have to be more complex, more like a living organism, with lines of authority and consultation and coordination crisscrossing in an intricate network of small units.

One area of operation in which everybody in an enterprise has a stake and some specialized knowledge is recruitment, training, and advancement of personnel. These issues, once wholly under management control, then increasingly a concern of union contracts, are now more and more affected by legislation, as society has concerned itself with the problems of poverty, racial discrimination and equal opportunity. Here, surely, is an area for imaginative innovation in devising procedures which will give those whose lives are most directly affected the chance to express themselves as citizens of the enterprise. Making decisions by majority vote, the traditional concept even of industrial democracy, is only one technique among many that may be found applicable within an enterprise.

Furthermore, the enterprise does not exist in a vacuum but is a part of a larger community.

More immediately affected by an enterprise even than its customers may be its next door neighbors. A plant makes decisions which affect housing, schooling, health care and similar issues, and the neighborhood should have a voice where its interests are affected. Conversely, workers in a plant have interests in the community where it is located, as well as in the community where they live. Such varied matters as water pollution, access to highways, recreational facilities, United Fund drives, are of concern both to an enterprise and to the surrounding community.

Looking farther afield to the larger community, a business or industry, and therefore all those engaged in it, may affect the lives of millions of others. A clear case, now widely recognized, is the automobile industry, with its products poisoning the air. To take another example, should the employees of Dow Chemical have anything to say about its manufacture of napalm? If we are all members one of another, should we not share the responsibilities as well as the benefits and burdens of our common efforts?

Most of these issues of large-scale business and industrial management, from internal housekeeping and the technical decisions of every working day to community relations, are as important to public enterprise as to private enterprise. Bureaucracy has the same face in a system calling itself socialist as under capitalism. Participatory democracy is as important in a government agency as in a private corporation, a charitable foundation, an international union, a veterans' organization, a church denomination, a hospital, or a university.

In the current time of unrest the university has been a particular target of the urge to share in decision-making.

12 | Participation in Learning

The demand for "student power" has divided the generations and made campuses into battlegrounds, but it is far more than simply the slogan of a few radicals. All over the country committees of middle-aged and young people are painfully hammering out new constitutions for the governance of educational institutions, and determining where and how students are to participate in running them. Even secondary schools are being forced by precocious teen-agers to answer similar questions.

As noted earlier, schools and colleges have hitherto largely escaped the democratic transformation which many other social institutions have undergone. An authoritarian structure has been taken for granted. The authoritarian model, to be sure, goes back to the biological fact that the human infant is helpless, and what the child learns as it grows up it learns from its more knowledgeable elders. Inequality is built into the relation between teacher and learner, as it is between parent and child. Traditionally the schoolmaster with his rod conditions his victims to accept discipline, and forces into their unwilling minds what they ought to know. In hierarchical societies education was limited to the ruling classes, and the more learned constituted an aristocracy, paralleling the aristocracy of arms.

Even after the democratic and egalitarian movements of the mod-

153

ern era brought in universal public education, authoritarian attitudes were carried over. Education was not simply made available to all, but it was made compulsory for all. Not until the reforms of "progressive" education at the turn of the century was the emphasis shifted back from the teacher to the learner.

Even then the institutional structure in which the learning process went on was not democratized. Many schools and colleges developed first as business enterprises. The schoolmaster was an entrepreneur. As private academies and colleges became larger and more complex, they tended to follow the pattern of the business corporation. Direction was entrusted to a board of trustees (directors) who in turn selected an executive manager. With the coming of public education the state or municipality represented ownership, and, at least in America, it appointed or elected the governing board. In the case of private, non-profit colleges and universities, the governing boards, responsible to no proprietor and only vaguely to governmental authorities, often became self-perpetuating. Day-to-day operations were entrusted by the board to administrators and faculty, who corresponded to the salaried executives of a business corporation.

In Europe the similarity to the business corporation may have been less than in America. Many universities antedated the industrial revolution. They were no less hierarchical, but the senior faculty rather than administrators were at the top of the pyramid. The European tradition helped faculties on American campuses to establish their academic independence of college and university administrations, and even to assume until recently that administrators would be selected from the faculty.

Yet as schools and colleges grew larger, staffs of non-teaching personnel—business managers, accountants, bookkeepers, secretaries, maintenance and housekeeping staffs—became necessary, and these have the same status as employees in any business corporation. Some have joined unions and won the same rights as industrial workers. But they obviously have had no significant opportunity to participate in governing the academic community.

And where were the students, the learners, for whose benefit the educational institution was ostensibly established? Following the analogy of the business corporation, they were the customers who purchased the educational product. Or, more accurately, their parents were the customers and paid for the product, either in the form of tuition charges or as taxes. The school was paid to take care of the training of the young not only in book learning but in manners and behavior. Even the university, which professed, in the European tradition, that it was a community of scholars, looked upon undergraduates as children to be instructed; even after they entered a professional school they were not considered citizens of a democratic and self-governing community.

In the contemporary tide of youthful disbelief and revolt, how can the student demand for a share in power be met? Probably a majority of the students are more interested in learning than they are in running the university, and their need to feel a part of an institution may be satisfied by supporting the football team. Those who do want active participation may find that the running of a university, like any large enterprise, offers varying possibilities of participation—or non-participation.

Most extra-curricular activities, like the social, athletic, and cultural programs available in some large businesses, have generally been left to the initiative and control of the participants. Even with football and other revenue-producing sports, students have shared control. Student publications have been increasingly free from censorship. In the making and enforcing of rules for student behavior and morals, the relinquishment of once absolute authority by college deans and presidents had begun long before the present campus revolt. Student government bodies were given increasing responsibility. Now the transfer of authority is becoming a stampede. After all, it is the students rather than the administration and faculty who have the primary interest in the behavior of their fellows. Yet some of the problems of these turbulent times may well make students hesitate to assume the full burden of governing themselves.

In the realm of sexual behavior, little regulation will be imposed by anybody. In the new freedom brought by changing moral standards

and "the pill," the individual student is increasingly considered entitled to make his or her own decisions. Similarly, whatever may be the
problems raised by the spreading use of drugs, they are not peculiar
to the campus, and "student power" is not likely to want much
responsibility for policing.

In two other areas of current student behavior, advocates of participatory democracy have difficult problems. One relates to the relatively new demand of black students for separate accommodations and
college facilities. Their white fellow students face the same dilemmas
as white administrators when confronted with that demand. The polarization of America into two societies, white and black, transcends
college concerns, and black separatism may well be a necessary stage
in overcoming the damage done by racial discrimination. Most decisions in this area may well have to be left to the black students
themselves. The greater the freedom granted black students to separate themselves from white students, the sooner are they likely to find
that separatism is sterile and even self-defeating. Democracy includes
the freedom to make mistakes.

The other problem is that of destructive and disruptive behavior.
How would students deal with violence if they shared responsibility
for maintaining order in a restructured university? Until the campus
revolt of the 1960's, student violence in this country was a matter of
football weekends and spring fever: deans, student councils and local
law enforcement authorities had no great difficulty in sharing responsibility when occasion arose. But today most destruction on campus has
been purposeful, connected with protests and demonstrations.

Some few campus radicals may believe that universities must be
totally destroyed, along with the power structure of which they are
part, in the cleansing fires of social revolution. Others engage in
disruptive or destructive activities in the belief that the resulting
reaction of the authorities will radicalize larger segments of the student body. More often, as suggested earlier, violence has been a
message which the perpetrators felt unable to get across in any other
way. Seizures of buildings, coercion of university officials, student
strikes and similar disruptive actions are the forms taken by protest

when the protestors feel the university belongs to the enemy.

There can be no guaranty against violence in the tensions of rapid and overdue change. But vandalism in college buildings would tend to be limited to the emotionally disturbed if the student body as a whole felt the campus was really theirs.

A man does not deface or damage his own home. A generation or two ago, even the columned porticos and ivied walls of the alma mater inspired a sentimental attachment. Fraternities built and maintained their own buildings, and their members were ready to do battle to defend them. In the restructuring of universities some of the same loyalties will emerge with self-government. If every dormitory and classroom building were to have its own elected house committee as many now do, then, even if only a few students were willing to take responsibility, at least the building might be less of a symbol of hostile authority. No massive protests would follow a call for police protection against vandals, and demonstrators armed with fire bombs would look for other targets.

For the most part, the operation and maintenance of the buildings and facilities in which an institution carries on its educational functions have been left to its business administration. Students may make an issue of the food in the cafeteria without wanting to assume responsibility for its management. They may protest the building of a gymnasium or the provision of athletic fields which run counter to their social conscience or political demands. Blacks and sympathetic whites may demand the hiring of more blacks, for example, on construction jobs. But the housekeeping aspects of a college campus, like that of any large enterprise, involve specialized knowledge or routine procedures with which most of the students will not want to be concerned. Still, all those affected—and by far the larger number, of course, are students—should have an opportunity to be heard, and to share in policy-making and supervision when so disposed.

Students usually take for granted the costly facilities provided by taxpayers or by the philanthropic munificence of older generations. So far, the demand for student power has not intruded significantly into the financial aspects of educational enterprises. Aside from protests against financial dependence on government grants for military research, the source of the money to operate and improve a university has been the least of the concerns of campus radicals. College presidents and administrators responsible for securing funds from state legislatures or federal agencies or alumni, and then for the complex problems of budgeting, allocating resources, and paying the bills, find it hard to be tolerant when students, instead of being grateful for the opportunities provided by other people's money, make truculent demands as to how it should be invested and how spent.

Yet financial decisions in an educational enterprise are not mere technical details. Tuition fees and charges, and the allocation of scholarships and grants in aid, are life and death matters to students; they should have an opportunity to be heard when schedules and procedures which may affect them are determined, and the individual should have all the safeguards against arbitrary action which constitute "due process" when the rules are applied to him. Similarly, on the major decisions involved in budgeting and appropriations, which determine the basic policies and programs of an institution, students can properly ask to be heard. If they are to be accepted as responsible citizens, they will sit on finance committees no less than on curriculum committees.

Decisions on what is taught, and by whom and how, have rested in a complex hierarchy of authorities, in which, traditionally, students have had no place. Over a public institution like the University of California, the Governor and the state legislature have the power to shape major policies and determine the personnel to carry them out. Private institutions may depend on church bodies or a shadowy constituency of alumni or a self-perpetuating board of trustees for long-range policy decisions. In any case, most academic policies and programs have been determined by school superintendents, college presidents, deans, department heads, and senior faculty members. The only broadening of the decision-making process has been, until recently, by giving faculties more voice. Even there, participation has been limited mainly to those faculty members who have been granted permanent tenure.

Now younger faculty members, graduate students who carry much of the teaching load, and students generally have revolted against this authoritarian pattern. The revolt started on those campuses with the greatest academic prestige, and has spread into almost every part of the educational system. It has been complicated by the black revolt, the peace movement and all the other turbulent currents of cultural change and social unrest. The underlying issue is the right of students to share in the control of their own education.

They are demanding and they are obtaining a voice, all the way from major policy decisions on the establishment of new departments such as black studies, and the relative emphasis to be given to teaching and research, to the content of particular courses. Beginning with opportunities to evaluate their professors, they are reaching out for a share in control of faculty appointments and promotions.

It is no wonder if college administrators with long experience in these areas resign in anger or despair, and regents or trustees find no one eager to take their places. It is no wonder if university professors, grown gray in their long struggle up the academic ladder, to the point where they are the proprietors and masters, and their students the transient customers, of their academic shop, now find it hard to accept their students as partners in a common process of learning.

Yet a teacher cannot teach except to students who want to learn. Ideally the motivation should be intellectual curiosity. More often it is because what is learned can be useful, particularly for earning a living. With vocational and professional students this objective is clear, and positive motivations are strong.

Unfortunately, more negative attitudes to learning are inculcated at an early age. Children are required to learn the three R's because society has no place for illiterates, and even if a child does not understand the relation between his education and his later earning capacity, his elders do. Rewards are remote, but penalties can be immediately imposed. While corporal punishment and the traditional birch rod are out of date, the age-old traditions which make a school a prison ruled by fear still linger, even at college levels.

The punishment for failure to do one's lessons is denial of the college degree without which entry into the affluent society is barred. The whole system of testing and grading tends to make the learning process bitter and painful for all but a few. This can perhaps be best seen in Asian universities established by former European colonial administrations, where the main activity is still a desperate struggle to pass examinations qualifying for jobs, as the only escape from grinding poverty. What their teachers are teaching and the students must learn may be wholly irrelevant, to be forgotten as soon as the examination is passed.

It is this kind of "rat race" against which the present student generation in this country has revolted, either by dropping out or by protesting and demonstrating. Whether they have learned enough self-discipline in the permissive atmosphere of modern upbringing to meet the requirements of modern technology may be questioned, but they clearly are not willing to be molded to the needs of corporate employers. They know the taste of freedom and decline to accept the traditional authoritarianism of the schools and colleges of their parents. Their demands, often shocking to their elders—for open admission to colleges and universities, "black studies" programs run by black students, abolition of grades and examinations, power over faculty appointments—may for a while lower academic standards. But their main thrust is to put the initiative for the learning process where it belongs, on the learners.

One of the products of campus unrest was the "people's university." It might have been no more than a dozen students meeting in a room on or off the campus, with a faculty member of their own choosing. It was likely to spring up during a period when regular classes in a university were shut down by a strike or disturbance. The faculty member might be a sympathetic younger member of the university faculty or he might be a radical black power advocate. Whoever he was, the students selected him because they wanted to learn what they believed he could teach them.

Sometimes students even met without a teacher. An enormous intellectual ferment went on during some of the sit-ins in university buildings. It has often been said that students can learn more from each other than from any professor. Even in normal times most of the learning in secondary schools and colleges takes place not in the classroom or the lecture hall but in individual study. If this can be combined with the mutual stimulus of discussion among equals, the amount of learning will be multiplied. Such education may not always meet the more exacting standards society must impose on those fields requiring special knowledge and technical skill, but it may be as important as any part of the educational process.

And it is almost certain to be more relevant. The major concern of those students who have demanded a share in the planning and programming of the educational process is that their education shall be relevant—relevant to their interests and needs and the world in which they find themselves. When higher education was the special preserve of the privileged and the ruling classes, many of whom had inherited wealth that obviated the need of learning a trade or profession, cultivation of the mind and esthetic taste through liberal arts and humanities programs was relevant enough. Many of today's students are dissatisfied with such an aim. They want to learn how to cope with the world confronting them.

This not only leads them to make demands for new kinds of studies but for new relations between the campus and the community. The effect of the university on housing and neighborhood amenities is not simply an issue raised by radical demonstrators in search of something to demonstrate about. It has a direct bearing on what a university actually is. Academic isolation, behind ivy-covered Gothic walls, was one of the luxuries of a society that thought itself "civilized," but it is meaningless for many of the new generation of college age. They want learning more intimately related to the local community. With new urban studies institutes, and more emphasis on extension courses, the learning process may well permeate the community.

Looking beyond the immediate neighborhood to the state and nation and the world, within which higher education must play an increasingly important role, it is clear how out of date the concept of the ivory tower is. The relation of the university to the development of weapons threatening the very existence of life on the planet has been clear enough since nuclear physicists started the first nuclear chain reaction at the University of Chicago more than a quarter of a century ago. Today, with half the population of the United States under twenty-five and at least half of these engaged in the educational process, it should not have been surprising that campuses became breeding grounds for revolutionary ideas. Even in the countries where the universities enroll a much smaller percentage of the young than in the United States today, they have been centers of disaffection making for social and political change.

Student power, without question, is here to stay. Some of its manifestations have been destructive, even cruel. But these are signs of immaturity—not so much the immaturity of the students participating, as immaturity in the development of the means and techniques by which the students can participate constructively.

13 The City as Neighborhood

M any of yesterday's young radicals who declared they would trust no one over thirty are reaching that age, if they have not already passed it. They are not, as their elders may have hoped, giving up their radical views. They are no more willing than they were to surrender control of their lives to some establishment for private or public power. Their belief that the entire society is rotten ripe for revolutionary change is as strong as ever, but they are more realistic in recognizing their own limitations and the complexity of the society they want to change.

Some have adopted as their own the increasingly widespread concern for the natural environment and its threatened destruction by pollution, overpopulation, and ruthless exploitation of resources. Others have been working with local and neighborhood organizations of protest and self-help. Often they feel that beyond any immediate benefits they may help achieve, they are building a new society within the framework of the old, a new structure ready to take over community functions at such time as the old system is overthrown or disintegrates.

Whether or not the revolution they anticipate ever takes place, at least in such a way that they will recognize it as a revolution, their instinct is sound: the hope for the big city lies in decentralizing its functions so that its citizens can once again become partners in self-governing neighborhoods and communities.

The word "community" carries a special significance. It is related to the word "commune," which so attracts the hippie world. But a commune is an escape, whereas the effort to develop a sense of true community in the neighborhood, through neighborhood enterprises and services, is a frontal attack on what is monstrous about the big city. The word "community" is also related to "communism," which still has a romantic appeal for the would-be revolutionist. But most of those who have been drawn to communist doctrines have discovered that communist subordination of means to ends has produced its own kind of tyranny in a self-perpetuating power structure.

So those of the new generation of radicals who are trying to realize the communal spirit in city neighborhoods are working in ways more consistent with their ultimate goals.

Any big city is a kind of big ghetto. Some areas may have expensive apartments or green-shaded streets, but they have some of the qualities of the overcrowded slum. The need to find personal significance in the sharing of significant community activity is too often thwarted.

The general principle to be applied in meeting the urban crisis should by now be apparent. The aim must be to break up the city into smaller, self-governing neighborhoods. No aggregation of people can be a true community unless it is on a scale small enough for the individual human being to feel that he counts.

It is ironic that the idea of community development was popularized in the poorer and less developed parts of the world, often with American aid, before it was applied to our own poor and undeveloped cities. Community development as it has been promoted in India, for example, focuses on the village. It enlists the active concern and participation of the villagers and their chosen leaders, in identifying problems of health, schooling, and the like, and assists them in organizing for their own self-help.

The process of lifting oneself by one's bootstraps is long and slow and often discouraging. But national governments and outside aid probably cannot bring the hundreds of millions of the Third World into the twentieth century except as the hundreds of thousands of villages go through the transforming processes of democracy on a small scale.

Perhaps the big city, including its ghettos, should be seen as a cluster of villages without visible boundaries. If the principles of community development are to be applied, the villages will have to be untangled and sorted out. This means recognizing the smaller units which already exist, defining their responsibilites, and giving them legitimacy. At the same time, as they become self-governing collective enterprises, they will have to be coordinated in complex federal patterns, if the larger governmental functions to be performed at district and regional and national levels are to be carried on.

In the war on poverty under the Economic Opportunity Act of 1964, the provision aimed most surely at the urban crisis was that of legitimizing neighborhood groups and giving them responsibility for community action programs. "Maximum feasible participation of the people to be served" had long been promoted by federal legislation in the farm aid programs, such as soil conservation districts and production controls, but had not been previously employed in programs for meeting city problems.

Neighborhood self-help in the ghetto, however, is not and should not be dependent on government programs. The black revolt, and the separatism that has emerged from black nationalism and pride in blackness, have prompted community enterprises in the ghettos, cultural, economic, and civic. Even the Black Panthers, despite their stated belief in the necessity of a revolution, have promoted a hot breakfast program for slum children as well as other community action programs. Underworld teen-age gangs have sometimes turned their energies into programs of civic improvement. In Chicago one of these gangs, the Blackstone Rangers, with the help of an unconventional Presbyterian church, has helped to give some of the residents of the city's South Side a feeling of greater security from crime.

And there are countless other examples of shared feelings and action in city neighborhoods.

If a general coordinated effort is to be made to decentralize our cities, to give their residents a feeling of genuine participation in significant group enterprises, the variety of function of those enterprises must be recognized and provided for.

The untangling of "villages" from the urban complex does not mean that their territorial boundaries will be defined in the same way for all purposes. Residents in an apartment building form a community for such common purposes as rent levels, heating, waste disposal, security. Residents of a block, or a neighborhood consisting of several blocks, have other common concerns, such as fire protection, noise abatement, a traffic light. Still other needs bring together even larger geographic areas, wards and districts within a city, and larger regions of which the city may be the center.

Geographic areas for different functions will not only be differently defined but will often overlap. A church of one denomination may serve an area quite unlike that of another church on the same street. It is common interest and common activity which define a community rather than set geographic boundaries.

Our big cities have grown out of small towns. A governmental function which can properly be handled on a municipal basis when a municipality is small may not be manageable in the same way when it has become big. Municipalities have traditionally had city-wide departments of education, public safety, welfare, public health and the like. If an effort is now to be made at decentralization, each of these governmental functions should be separately examined.

The neighborhood school is an object of violent emotion. In New York City bitter struggles occurred in the late 1960's between the locally elected governing boards of experimental school districts set up in three areas and the teachers union, with the city authorities caught in the middle. Each of those experimental school districts served an area as big as a medium-sized city. The neighborhoods, consisting mainly of blacks and Puerto Ricans, became involved in the schools, and the morale of parents, children, and specially selected and often youthful teachers was high.

Responding to the pressure, the state legislature acted to decentralize the entire city school system. While the autonomous districts already in existence protected their loss of identity, districts through-out the city elected their own boards and acquired a greater degree of local control. But the new districts may still be too large, as suggested by the low turnout for the district board elections. The process of decentralization may have to be carried even further.

Something reminiscent of the one-room schoolhouse of the New England village was re-created when groups of parents were assisted under Office of Economic Opportunity programs to set up a Head Start or day care center for a single housing development or small neighborhood: in addition to the benefits for their children, parents gained new stature as they became concerned and functioning citizens, responsible for their own community enterprises.

Could all elementary education be decentralized in the same way? Every primary school would then be a neighborhood community center, responsible to a locally elected school board. Conformity with municipal, state, and national standards for curricula, accreditation of teachers, absence of racial discrimination and the like, would be maintained as at present—as conditions for obtaining financial aid—but without lessening the feeling of the neighborhood residents that it was their school. Teachers pay-scales and other benefits would have to be settled by negotiation on a broader basis, but hiring would be a local function.

Even a single neighborhood school is a collection of smaller groups, grades, and classes. A classroom full of children, their parents and their teachers, forms a group with a common interest, engaged in a common enterprise. In matters of discipline and schoolroom environment and procedures, they may be better qualified for decision-making even than a community school board. In the Soviet Union, the idea of a Parent Teacher Association for each school has been carried a step further by educational experimenters, and parents of children in each schoolroom are supposed to meet periodically, to advise and consult on the learning process.

At high school level the small neighborhood school is no longer practicable. In New England, small rural school districts are encouraged to join forces in regional high schools, and a similar pattern of small-scale federalism could be followed in a city that had decentralized its educational system down to the neighborhood level.

Resistance to school decentralization naturally comes from established educational hierarchies, and from teachers' unions which have at long last won economic security for their members through collective bargaining. But there is no inherent contradiction between local autonomy and the exercise of certain powers at higher levels.

One serious dilemma presented by school decentralization must be recognized: it is difficult to see how community control and elimination of de facto segregation can be simultaneously accomplished in large cities so long as the neighborhoods themselves are segregated. The answer of course is to break up the segregated housing patterns and to achieve integrated neighborhoods, but this will require massive effort and cannot be done overnight. For the short run, different communities may set different priorities. In some, the elimination of segregated schools may seem to be the overriding imperative; in others, especially the very large cities with immense ghetto areas, community control may emerge as the more immediate and practical objective.

If community control of education is important for the ghetto, community control of the police is even more so. Nothing has caused greater tension and bitterness than the feeling that the police are an enemy force, serving an alien power structure in the name of law and order. Slum dwellers are the principal victims of crime, yet municipal police forces often seem to be more interested in the protection of wealthier areas.

The report of the Kerner Commission on Civil Disorders pointed out various ways in which police departments could become more responsive to the sensibilities and needs of ghetto residents, and suggested that local residents and part-time volunteers might perform some police functions. The commission did not, however, fully examine the possibilities of decentralizing the police function.

Crime of course does not respect neighborhood boundaries, but we may have been too much concerned with the professional criminal and organized crime, and insufficiently aware of the extent to which crime is a local problem. Why should not local neighborhoods have primary responsibility for their own law and order? The fact that this is a Black Panther demand should not be cause for rejection. Industrial and business establishments have their own security forces. Many apartment houses and housing developments, faced by mounting urban crime, now do the same. University campuses have jealously guarded their right to police themselves. If rural communities can appoint their own constables, why not city neighborhoods? In each case municipal or state police will still be available for those protective and law enforcement functions that cannot be handled locally.

Ghetto residents, victims no less than perpetrators of crime, see the police chiefly in terms of harassment and repression. There is no more explosive ingredient in the ghetto than resentment of police brutality and racial prejudice, and no more urgent issue than the availability of redress. Civilian review boards have been urged to assure independence in investigation of complaints, but, even more important than their civilian composition, such review boards should include local residents able to interpret and reflect the feelings of the community.

Decentralization of the police, as of schools, will begin to make possible, even in the big city, the kind of local self-government enjoyed by the small rural community. There are no insuperable obstacles to decentralizing other municipal departments. The supposed economies of centralized administration of roads and highways, for instance, might disappear if one more closely examined the overgrown bureaucracies which cluster around city hall, even when municipal government is enlightened and honest. Why not give the neighborhood responsibility for maintenance and repair of those streets which serve only the neighborhood?

Many public services, to be sure, cannot be provided locally. Some, such as water and sewage disposal, public utilities and transport, may even depend on larger units than the municipality, and metropolitan districts and regions for various purposes may be needed.

Public health also transcends local boundaries, but hospital districts and clinical facilities can be largely under local control. In the field of mental health, the huge and remote mental hospital is now properly out of favor, and more attention is being given to the need for local out-patient mental health clinics. These provide additional opportunities for participation by local planning and consulting groups and individual volunteers. State and federal aid programs in recent years have encouraged local initiative in these areas.

Another function that ought to be at least partly decentralized in operation, if not in financing, is assistance for those unable to support themselves. While the trend is clearly in the direction of greater federal government responsibility to carry the financial burden of welfare and of a minimum income program, yet many of life's emergencies and vicissitudes call for special consideration beyond the mere provision of a set amount of money. The role of the city and state will continue, but local welfare agencies, both public and private, are also essential if individual needs are to be fully met and human dignity respected. Neighborly concern is still a vital factor in the big city.

As government functions are decentralized, new governmental or quasi-governmental districts are created. A resident of a suburban or rural area is already accustomed to the idea of belonging to different, and often overlapping, jurisdictions—a fire district, a water district, a police district, and so on. He is also likely to be familiar with the imposition of separate taxes to cover the cost of each separate local service, though a county or state tax-collecting authority may send him only one combined bill.

Many local government functions must, of course, be subsidized in whole or in part by county, state, or federal authorities, but if a local community or neighborhood is to have significant decision-making power it must be more than merely an administrative unit of a far-flung bureaucracy: it must be able to raise and spend its own money. Decision-making is likely to be mere shadowboxing if someone else totally controls the purse. The power to tax is a sovereign power, but states are already accustomed to delegating it not only to cities and towns and boroughs, but to special districts and even neighborhood associations.

In some cities neighborhood associations have been formally organized as membership corporations, with an assembly composed of all local residents who care to sign up as members and an elected executive council. Such a neighborhood corporation is a flexible and versatile vehicle for all kinds of decision-making. The corporation can oversee and operate social programs, perform services on a contract basis, promote and assist local business enterprises, and perform such governmental functions as may be delegated to it. A federation of many such corporations would enjoy considerable political muscle, even in a large city, and would be able to negotiate effectively with City Hall.

Many group activities that are important to the vitality of a community are non-governmental, and are not supported out of taxes. Association with them may be unrelated to any defined geographical area. Dwellers in the ghetto and in the suburbs, no less than in rural areas, may belong to a variety of organizations—churches, clubs, tenants councils, block and neighborhood associations, union locals. Voluntary participation is the life blood of most of the organizations and associations which cater to common economic social and cultural interests. Some give their members more opportunity for active participation than others, but even such an ancient, authoritarian institution as the Roman Catholic Church has begun to be affected by the democratic tide. In these voluntary associations many people find the main substance and meaning of their lives; here decentralization is already in effect.

Any over-all policy of community development, to counter the vast inhumanity and depersonalization of the big city, must give the voluntary association fullest scope. So also must it support the decentralization and transformation of the business corporation and the shops and offices where people spend their working lives, if their creative energies are to be released.

There is no simple solution to the urban crisis. The effort to make life in a big city one of significant participation in common enterprises commonly valued depends on creating opportunities that have hitherto only been found, under ideal conditions, in a village or small town.

Yet opportunity to participate should not imply obligation. Modern life is so complex, and the group activities which affect our lives are so infinite in number, that in most of them, for most of the time, only a few of us would want to take active part. The freedom not to participate is as important as the freedom to participate. Experience with community action programs under the OEO, as with the efforts to give university students a voice in university policy, has demonstrated that most people do not want to be burdened with the responsibilities of power once they are made available. Yet if they are not to feel helpless victims, they must be able to take part when they want to, and to have close contact with those who do.

The oppressive nature of the big city must and will be transformed. If the urban crisis is not met constructively it will be resolved with fury and destruction. To make our monstrous overgrown cities into pleasant dwelling places for the life and work of human beings will call for all the creative imagination, inventive capacity and sophisticated technology that man can bring to bear.

14 | The World as Neighborhood

W hen Norman Mailer applied his dramatic insights as a novelist to the problems of New York and ran for mayor, his gesture may have been politically naïve, but his concepts of a federation of autonomous neighborhoods, and of New York City not merely as a municipality but as a sovereign state, were valid and provocative.

The concept of new towns planned and created with only the natural features of the landscape to limit them represents another bold leap into the future. The largest of these is Columbia, now growing in the remaining open space between Washington and Baltimore. Like an earlier model, the Australian capital city of Canberra, it applies the valuable principle of multiple federalism: a city as a cluster of villages, each a cluster of neighborhoods.

It is only through a growing multiplicity of decision-making bodies, not only in towns, cities, and neighborhoods, but at the state and national level, and even beyond the state and nation, that the individual can hope to become a truly participatory citizen.

The United States is already more than merely a federation of states, it is today increasingly a federation of federations, a complex network of more or less self-governing units. In addition to state governments and the local governments of counties, cities, and towns, governmental powers are exercised by a variety of functional regions and

districts: soil conservation districts, river valley authorities, port authorities, judicial districts, Federal Reserve districts, planning regions,
and many others. The national body politic also includes many non-
governmental federations, representative bodies of autonomous units,
chambers of commerce, labor unions, professional associations. Ours
is a highly pluralistic society, a community of communities.

There is salvation in such diversity, even though diversity means
extreme complexity. The executive mentality prefers simplicity. It
sees efficiency in simple and clear lines of authority. Political purists
have often tried to improve government operations by eliminating
overlapping and duplication in public agencies, and no doubt such
pruning and streamlining of public administration is a continuing
need. But if hundreds of millions are to have a perceptible role in
governing themselves, it will have to be as members of hundreds of
thousands of decision-making bodies. The more of such governmental
and quasi-governmental bodies there are, the more people can participate in the decisions that affect them.

Obviously, no matter how great the pluralism, no matter how exten-
sive the decentralization, many of the most important governmental
decisions will continue to have to be made at higher levels, through
the processes of representative, rather than direct, democracy. One of
the basic reasons for today's unrest is the widespread feeling that this
machinery is no longer responsive—if indeed it ever was—to the needs
and desires of the individual citizen. The list of grievances is a long
one: it includes, for example, the system of handing inordinate power
to congressional committee chairmen who hold their posts by virtue
only of seniority and who are out of sympathy with their own party's
policies. Another source of justified resentment is the growing expense
of political campaigning, which makes it virtually impossible for a
poor person to gain elective office, and which gives undue influence
to the lobbies that make generous campaign contributions.

City minority groups feel frustrated, prevented by gerrymandering
from having fair representation in legislative bodies. Country people
likewise may feel their interests ignored because the application of the
"one man, one vote" principle has deprived small towns and rural

areas of their representatives in state and county legislative bodies.

These and many other flaws impair the prestige of our political system, particularly among young people who see no reason to take inherited institutions for granted. But such flaws are not inherent. They can be corrected, and no doubt they will be. The speed and direction of reforms will depend in large measure on the degree to which the energy now dissipated in alienation and generalized anger can be directed toward the achievement of specific goals.

No doubt one reason for the relative lack of interest in specific governmental reforms until now has been the sense of impending doom that afflicts the generation now rebelling. It is an unhappy generation, early conditioned to despair. With millions of other TV viewers, it has seen the earth from the sterile lunar landscape lost in infinite space, a blue-green ball swathed in mists: though pulsating with life, it is ticking like a time bomb, and may one day become an atomic wasteland as lifeless as the moon. If we swarming end-products of organic evolution do not kill each other outright, we may suffocate in our own numbers, buried in our own waste. Whether our civilization ends with a bang or a whimper, the effect will be the same. Our talent for governing ourselves will have lagged too far behind our other talents.

Yet this grim picture, made familiar by dozens of writers of science fiction, is perhaps as falsely conceived as the more utopian vision of a previous generation which foresaw eternal progress toward a kingdom of God on earth. We don't know enough of man's potential to forecast his ability or inability to adjust to his environment. There are positive and hopeful trends as well as dangers.

Behind the politics of power and confrontation and all the arsenals of fiendish weapons lurks the almost universal belief that man should live in brotherhood with his fellow man. That belief is now reinforced by the growing conviction that he must, if he is to live at all.

The rebel generation of today is perhaps the first to realize fully that the concept of national sovereignty is dangerously out of date and that the world is a single community. But the rebels are as little impressed with what they see of the world's institutions as they are with their own national institutions. The United Nations, usually incapable of coping with the world's worst trouble spots, offers little inspiration.

Unhappily, nationalism is stronger in the world today than it was in 1945. If we were setting out now to create an international peace-keeping organization, we would probably not do as well as the founding fathers of the U.N. did in San Francisco.

If effective world government is not attainable, however, despair and total passivity are not the only alternatives. On the international front, as on the local and national level, there is much that can be done to strengthen and improve the institutions we have. Again, the most promising course is in the direction of multiplicity and variety of institutions, rather than a monolithic power structure.

There is already a host of functional organizations, both within and outside the U.N. system, through which the peoples of the world carry on their common affairs. Long before the League of Nations was founded, the Universal Postal Union was established. International efforts to control communicable diseases led eventually to the creation of the World Health Organization. The International Labor Organization, in which labor and management are at least theoretically represented, as well as governments, has been engaged since 1919 in promoting improved working conditions. Other world organizations deal with agriculture, education, industry, trade, money and banking, atomic energy, civil aviation, shipping, communications, weather forecasting. An agency to license exploitation of the ocean bottom may be next. The list will keep growing.

In addition, there is an increasing number of regional organizations. Like their worldwide counterparts, they have so far been more effective in achieving economic cooperation than in limiting political sovereignty. But the habit of working together is being acquired.

Of possibly even greater importance are the innumerable international organizations that bring together representatives of private interests—scientific, artistic, cultural, religious, commercial—whenever human intercourse transcends national boundaries. Among the oldest of these are the Olympic games and the Roman Catholic Church.

One such group, operating in a field of supreme importance, is the committee for the Pugwash Conferences. Named for the Nova Scotia town where the first was held, these conferences have brought together leading scientists from both sides of the Iron Curtain to consider how scientific genius may be shifted from devising ever more terrible weapons toward building a better world.

The world's great religions have always proclaimed the gospel of human brotherhood, and today more religious people than ever before see the need for renouncing power politics and racial bias and look toward world unity. Relief organizations like the International Red Cross and Caritas have dealt with disaster and famine in the tradition of the Good Samaritan. Even national governments offer succor, not alone for national advantage, but also out of a real sense of a common humanity.

Thousands of organizations and millions of people are engaged in undertakings that give form to that common humanity. One that exemplifies the new spirit is the Peace Corps, and many of its volunteers have returned to America determined to bring about needed changes at home.

The words *politics, policy, police,* and *polite* all come from *polis,* the self-governing city state of ancient Greece. The Latin words for citizen, *civis,* and for city, *urbs,* give us not only *civilization* and *urbanization* but *civility* and *urbanity.* Cities and states must use force to defend themselves against internal or external enemies, but their everyday social cement is mutual respect and a common feeling of belonging together. Our very language argues that the vitality and durability of a social group depend as much on manners as on force.

Such social cement is more obvious in a small group, the family, the neighborhood, the small town or village community, the voluntary association or social club. But the same sense of belonging to and being loyal to a community is a major ingredient of national patriotism. And a generation is now growing up who feel their first loyalty is to the human family.

Our most acute troubles today stem from the big city, and the military confrontation of the great nation states. There is barbarism rather than civility in both areas. Our survival, collectively as a species and individually as truly human beings, may depend on our developing the feeling—and institutions to sustain the feeling—of belonging to a neighborhood and participating in its affairs: this is the more difficult because our neighborhood for some purposes is megalopolis and for others the whole world. We will need all the discipline demanded of our computers if we are to make either neighborhood a pleasant place to live. We may also need all that we can muster of tolerance and hope.

Pessimism is the order of the day. A climate of violence seems to have crept over America, as it has over most of the world. Rising rates of violent crime, addiction to violence on television and in entertainment, an obsessive accumulation of ever more diabolical weapons, and increasing civil disorder, all suggest a sick society, a return to savagery, a replay of the overthrow of Rome by the barbarians. Yet an optimist can point out that no civilized society ever showed more humane concern for the welfare of the weak and helpless or held individual human life of greater worth. Capital punishment is all but abolished. The treatment of the mentally ill is under far-reaching reform. New behavioral sciences are attacking social ills long thought out of reach. The population explosion is not only widely recognized for the first time as a deadly threat, but its control has been made feasible through a revolutionary change in public attitudes. Similarly, other problems which at first may seem intractable, such as environmental pollution and depletion of resources, hunger, national pride and racial intolerance, are being newly recognized—a first, and indispensable step, toward ultimate solutions. Beyond all these, the feeling that we are all one human family has never before been so universal or so strong.

No organized society can tolerate more than a certain level of disorder. The romantic revolutionist may dream of a society without a policeman, but if he acts out his dreams he may well find he has provoked a police state that is no fantasy. On the other hand, a dynamic, pluralistic society like ours, while maintaining order in a rule of law, must expect and allow for a measure of disorder. Only a repressive authoritarian society or dictatorship can hope to appear always peaceful, orderly and law-abiding.

The turbulence of the past decade is the restlessness not of a sick but of a healthy society. Its troubles are real enough and could prove fatal, but they are the stresses and strains of growth and change in a society of unprecedented affluence and unprecedented freedom.

That freedom has, of course, no guaranty of permanence. But it is not so much threatened by the turbulence of the young, even when they plot revolution or show a disregard for rights and privileges won at great cost by earlier generations. The danger comes rather from a panicky reaction of the Establishment to restlessness run riot. If both sides lose their cool, revolt could make of violence a self-fulfilling prophecy. Signs of a more repressive mood are all too evident.

Yet there are also signs that the generation gap is closing, that the older members of society are becoming more open to change, and that young people are becoming more aware of real opportunities to be creative.

Creative effort, like birth, is painful. Freedom to make decisions is not to be found in the Garden of Eden. But with the help of a saving sense of proportion all kinds of people can learn how to get along together—and even enjoy it.

Index